THE PATH OF PURPOSE

SHIFTING FROM DESTINATION TO JOURNEY

Aaron McDaniel

Copyright © 2021 Aaron McDaniel.

All rights reserved. No part of this book may be used or reproduced by any means, graphic, electronic, or mechanical, including photocopying, recording, taping or by any information storage retrieval system without the written permission of the author except in the case of brief quotations embodied in critical articles and reviews.

This book is a work of non-fiction. Unless otherwise noted, the author and the publisher make no explicit guarantees as to the accuracy of the information contained in this book and in some cases, names of people and places have been altered to protect their privacy.

WestBow Press books may be ordered through booksellers or by contacting:

WestBow Press
A Division of Thomas Nelson & Zondervan
1663 Liberty Drive
Bloomington, IN 47403
www.westbowpress.com
844-714-3454

Because of the dynamic nature of the Internet, any web addresses or links contained in this book may have changed since publication and may no longer be valid. The views expressed in this work are solely those of the author and do not necessarily reflect the views of the publisher, and the publisher hereby disclaims any responsibility for them.

Any people depicted in stock imagery provided by Getty Images are models, and such images are being used for illustrative purposes only.
Certain stock imagery © Getty Images.

Interior Image Credit: Arch Bridges." Arch, 2004,
www.warwickallen.com/bridges/ArchBridges.htm.

Scripture quotations taken from The Holy Bible, New International Version® NIV® Copyright © 1973 1978 1984 2011 by Biblica, Inc. TM. Used by permission. All rights reserved worldwide.

Scripture taken from the King James Version of the Bible.

Scripture taken from The Message. Copyright © 1993, 1994, 1995, 1996, 2000, 2001, 2002. Used by permission of NavPress Publishing Group.

ISBN: 978-1-6642-3626-4 (sc)
ISBN: 978-1-6642-3627-1 (hc)
ISBN: 978-1-6642-3628-8 (e)

Library of Congress Control Number: 2021911263

Print information available on the last page.

WestBow Press rev. date: 07/29/2021

CONTENTS

Ackowledgements vii

CHAPTER 1 1
Failure on the Path 3
Patience on the Path 20
Foundation of the Path 28
Confidence on the Path 45
Stamina on the Path 57
Isolation on the Path 73
Peace on the Path 80
Brokenness on the Path 88
Dependency on the Path 101
Choice of the Path 116
Fear of the Purpose 123
Testimony of the Path 131
Path Prayers 136

Works Cited 139

ACKOWLEDGEMENTS

To my wife, Jillian. The first reader of this book and the first editor. Without you, none of these sentences would even be legible. To say that I appreaciate your support throughout the process of this book would an incredible understatement. You are my life partner and my best friend. I love you, Jilly.

To my Mom, Dad, and dear friend, Bruce Terry. Thank you for reading the hot mess of this book that was my first draft. You all encouraged me and helped me make the book what it is. Thank you sincerely.

CHAPTER 1

This actually isn't the first chapter. It's the introduction. But if you're like me, you would have skipped right over this had you seen the word *introduction* at the top of this page. I mean, if it should be part of the book, why is it called *introduction* and separated from the rest of the book? Am I right?

I won't keep you long here. I just wanted to tell you why I wrote this book and why you should read it. I've always heard people say things like, "No matter how hard life gets, just don't worry. It will work out if you love God." Many times, people acknowledge there are difficult circumstances but only talk about the beginning and the end. People acknowledge problems exist and there will be a conclusion. While that is true, may I just point out that saying things like, "Don't worry. It'll work out" helps no one who is actually going through difficult seasons in life? Yes, I understand that one day all this may work out, but how do I get through this season? How do I get through the day to day of the incredibly difficult times? How do I keep walking when I can't? How do I have faith when I honestly don't? How do I have purpose when I feel like there isn't one?

To be as blunt as possible, sometimes life is brutal. And sometimes even the good days are politely described as difficult. I'm not trying to be a pessimist; I'm just trying to be vulnerable and honest.

The point of writing this book is to uncover the lies we can tend to believe in difficult seasons and hopefully encourage you to shift your focus from the difficulties and problems to God. Romans 10:17 says,

> *Faith comes from hearing the message, and the message*
> *is heard through the word about Christ.*

That being said, the goal throughout this book is to talk about the difficult seasons of life through the lens of the Word of God so our difficult seasons and problems are filtered through faith to stand on a solid foundation—a foundation that isn't affected by the seasons we walk through.

People love to talk about how you have a purpose, how to discover your purpose, how your purpose is important, but few want to talk about how to live that out. And I don't mean, "How do you get to the place of life where your every day is full of glory and peace?" I mean, "How do you live out your purpose when your life feels miserable, unfair, or impossible?"

Let's talk about it.

FAILURE ON THE PATH

THE EXPECTATION OF FAILURE

Failure. Not good enough. Can't measure up. You lost. Someone else is better. Loser.

These are all words we've either thought about ourselves or that have been spoken into our lives. Failure is the one thing in our lives that makes everyone uncomfortable. If you don't know much about me—I'm not sure why you would because this is my first book and I'm not famous—I am from the great state of Alabama. Here in Alabama, we're familiar with college football championships (Roll Tide). The head coach of that great team that brings home the championships is one Mr. Nick Saban. I heard Coach Saban say, "If I have another season where I lose three games, I think [these fans] will kill me" (author's paraphrase). That's the level of expectation and standard of excellence that has been set. It isn't fair, honestly, to the head coach that there is such a standard. A few folks may remember this, but before Mr. Saban, there wasn't a lot of winning happening down in what many now call Title Town. The Crimson Tide fans were blown away when we would sneak in that eighth win of the season! Now there is a different standard to live up to, and the man who set the standard has to continually deliver that standard. Anything less than meeting that standard is considered a failure. Mr. Saban made the organization successful, and he is undeservingly repaid with severe scrutiny. Understand, please, that I am not on a soapbox here. I am simply pointing out that it's interesting the "wins" that were once a blessing to those around us have now become an expectation.

I say all that to say this: your failure is always highlighted most by those who support you. This is a critical concept because if we take all the words that are said to heart by our supporters and allow them to weigh us down, we can prematurely leave a position we are called to be in. I'm not saying we shouldn't take counsel when it is due, but it's difficult to continue to stay in a situation where our failures are highlighted more than we would like. It can be draining to wake up every day to perform based on another's expectation as the definition of, whether or not our lives are successful. But this is the key that unlocks failure in your life. You can only fail when expectations are not met, and they unfortunately are typically set by those around us. So we "fail" simply whenever expectations set by our "supporters" are not met. We begin to carry this burden of trying not to fail to an extent that the burden consumes all of our thoughts and actions. This drains us, and we leave a position we are called to be in. Understand this, though: the expectations are never going to stop or even slow down. We have to understand how to learn through the failure—learning lessons, if you will.

IS FAILURE LEARNING?

If you live and breathe—which, if you're reading this book, is highly probable—there is an opportunity to learn through failure every day. I say *every day* because if we are truly trying to grow, there is a growing pain to deal with. And if we are growing every day, would it not make sense that there is a growing pain, or lesson, to go with it? There's always an opportunity to grow because, since we are human, failure will always be in our lives.

Many people live frustrated lives because they can't shake failure. In the center of our beings, we have a spiritual opposition to face every day, and if you get into the ring enough times, losing may be in your near future. If losing isn't your thing, kudos.

Now let me just talk to the normal people for a while. We can't be surprised when opposition comes to us at any given moment. John Maxwell wrote in his book *Developing the Leader within You 2.0* about the oppositions of life. He references a book by M. Scott Peck that states, "Once we truly know that life is difficult—once we truly understand and accept it—then life is no longer difficult."[4] When I read this for the first time, I had to stop and reevaluate my life. I had spent so long burdened by all my failures, and this one sentence revealed I was viewing the entire concept of failure totally wrong.

From a young age, we are taught to avoid failure. Note that avoiding is not synonymous with defeating. Growing up, I played the typical sports—baseball, football, and basketball—and I tried soccer one time. The soccer thing didn't go so well. Apparently, it's not cool to catch the ball. Whatever. No matter what sport I was playing, my dad would always send me out with this encouragement: "Play like you're playing to win. Don't play like you're playing not to lose." In other words, don't play in fear of messing up, but play as if you can't mess up.

So many times, we enter a season of our lives just hoping not to mess it up. We have zero care to actually grow and enhance our lives when opposition arrives. If we are honest, the end goal is simply to come out on the other side no worse than when we entered. Again not defeat but avoid. The brutal truth is you will be different when you come out of a season. How you exit the season is up to you. Coming out the other side of failure different is easy, but coming out the other side of failure *better* is difficult. I say it's difficult to come out better because it requires a mindset change. Every season and every day has opposition. Opposition, then, develops a trial—a testing, if you will.

Back in college, testing days did not come exactly easily for me. I would spend days preparing for an exam, all to make a 30 on a midterm that had nothing to do with what I studied. Does this mean that I instantly failed college? Thank God that it doesn't. Was it a moment of opposition? Yes, for sure. I graduated college, somehow by the grace of our Lord Jesus, so you could say that overall I was victorious. My mom will joke that my wife graduated magna cum laude while I graduated "thank the *Lawde.*" Anyway, in the moment of taking an exam I knew nothing about (and I seriously mean nothing; I was floored that I even got a 30), I felt like a failure. That is not an easy burden to deal with, especially for a perfectionist. Let me pose this question: If a quarterback throws an interception, does he immediately lose the game? My point is that failure can even found be in the victories. There will always be failure, and if we learn from the failures instead of beating ourselves up, growth happens.

THE SIGNIFICANCE OF FAILURE

Look at Moses. He was a stand-up guy. He'd be one of the four chiseled faces on the Mount Rushmore of the Bible. We'd all love to be as significant as Moses, but Moses's significance and authority came long after humble beginnings. Moses began his life floating down a crocodile-filled river all because the government wanted him and all the new Israelite babies dead (Exodus 1, Exodus 2:3). Still want to be a significant player like Moses?

Ironically, Moses was discovered by Pharaoh's daughter, who sheltered and nurtured him in the same place that was trying to kill him (Exodus 2:5). Even though this may not seem like a fairy tale, God was beginning to develop Moses's purpose. Growing older, Moses witnesses an Egyptian brutally whipping an Israelite slave and decides to secretly take action. Moses thought it over and concluded that killing the Egyptian would probably resolve the issue. Moses then murders the Egyptian (Exodus 2:12).

The next day, a fellow Hebrew calls him out for murder. When Pharaoh hears word, he tries to end Moses's life for the second time. Moses flees (Exodus 2:15). Now, I'm not sure where you're at in life, but more than likely, you are not trying to escape someone trying to kill you because you murdered a guy. If you are, your life seems a bit more exciting than mine.

This moment of failure in Moses's life leads him to another moment: a holy moment forty years later, when God tells Moses to go back to Egypt (Exodus 3:10).

> *So now, go. I am sending you to Pharaoh to bring my people the Israelites out of Egypt.*

God sends Moses back to the place that rejected him—back to where he failed to fulfill his purpose. What does all of this in Moses's life mean? It means that there is a purpose in the failure. Moses was primed to be a leader of Egypt; he was in line to be an authority over those who enslaved his people. How easy would it have been for Moses to fulfill his purpose to overthrow Egypt while sitting on a throne *in* Egypt? How simple would it have been to free the people he rules over? It would have saved God some inconvenience, don't you think? But Moses failed. He went from a prince of Egypt to Egypt's most wanted in just a moment—in just one action. It seems a bit absurd that the man called to liberate God's people would now be exiled from the exact place he was supposed to fulfill God's purpose. The story seems like it should be over. It's like watching your favorite Netflix show and not understanding why Lorelai just can't be with Luke;[5] it all seems a bit helpless at this point.

Go along with me for a minute. If you can, find a Bible and pick it up. Now turn to Exodus 2. You are now reading the chapter where Moses had his ultimate failure and completely messed up God's purpose for his life. Now, turn to Deuteronomy 34. This is where the story of Moses ended. Just look at how many pages are in your hands.

You see, Moses's purpose wasn't over when he failed. Neither is yours. There is still purpose past your failure.

Moses may have thought his failure ruined everything, but God knew something Moses didn't. If Moses never faces the horrible failure found in his killing the Egyptian, Moses never flees his home. If he never flees, then he never goes into an isolated foreign place. Moses actually felt so isolated that he named his son Gershom which means, "I have become a foreigner in a foreign land" (Exodus 2:22). If Moses was never isolated, He could never hear the burning bush. If he never hears and responds to that burning bush, he doesn't fulfill the purpose God placed on his life; ultimately, the people of Israel would never become free. Even in what looks like failure, there is still purpose. God may not be in charge of the actions that lead to failure, but He does work His purpose into our lives despite the failure. Sometimes, purpose comes through failure. Even when you don't understand, even when your life makes no sense, there's still purpose. God has a way of making everything work together to prosper those who are called by His name for His Kingdom.

THIS ISN'T WHAT I THOUGHT IT WOULD BE

Often in the journey of our path, it's easy to get fixated on the finish line. That's only natural. There is a purpose God has called you to, and you want to fulfill it—nothing wrong with that. However, in the middle of the path, we must be patient. Just like Moses, we won't be able to walk out our purpose in the correct authority if we do not allow God to correctly position us first. To quote John Maxwell again, he says, "Too many people want to know the end of the story before they are willing to take the first step."[4] This is a common mindset that will only bring frustration to your walk with Christ. He asks us to walk by faith (2 Corinthians 5:7). Because of this know-before-you-go mentality, so many people become frustrated during the walk with Christ due to their fixation of the end result.

Think back on your high school days real quick. What formed you into the person you are? Was it the one day of graduation or all the mundane school days that led up to you walking across the auditorium stage? If we don't have contentment in where we are on our path of purpose, fixating on the end goal can make the mundane days feel like constant failures. We can take teaching moments from God and turn them into self-beatings because we won't allow those moments to teach us the perseverance necessary to become what God has called us to be. This mentality will keep you in such a frustrated state. This mindset of living is why most do not walk into their purpose. The level of constant frustration of failing develops insecurity in who we are called to be in Christ. Instead of hearing what God is teaching us, we develop a fixated frustration with what we are *not* instead of what we are becoming. We stay so bogged down in lies, self-pity, and hopelessness that we unconsciously give up on the end goal, never fulfilling our purpose. We forget to see the big picture of God's sovereign plan and how our failures fit perfectly into His design.

Let's break this down for a minute. When in any biblical story has the promise of God developed simply and without frustration? Look at Abraham, Moses, Noah, and Joseph. In each of their lives, God designed a purpose, and they walked blindly in faith when everyone else around them said that they would be failures. Abraham left everything he had to be a father of many nations. Not just a father of many children but of nations. And he was an old man that wasn't even close to having a child. Moses was supposed to walk up to a king and ask for his slaves to be let go and to be snappy about it. Noah was supposed to build a boat when the ground wasn't even damp. Joseph was sold by his family and waiting for God to show up in prison. Do you need any more convincing? God rarely works things out the way our minds expect them. When our expectations aren't met, we begin to doubt if God even called us; maybe, we even begin to panic and label ourselves as failures. The journey through the path of our purpose is difficult and long. We're on the path because God called us by His promise in the first place. He has guided our steps (Proverbs 16:9).

> *In their hearts humans plan their course, but the Lord establishes their steps.*

However, the murky middle part of the path becomes weary and tiring; voices swarm, attempting to grab our attention. We begin to give validation to those doubts; the voices fault us for the promise of God not being fulfilled yet. Lies are planted in our minds convincing us that since we cannot understand why things have turned out the way they have, we must not be in the right place. We open the door to be convinced that these lies are solid truth to stand on. There is one problem with that: lies are like quicksand, and we will not only be stuck in where we are, but we will suffocate. It's difficult in the middle to have as much faith as we did when we began, but that's when faith is built—when we can't see (2 Corinthians 5:7).

> *For we live by faith, not by sight.*

We may not understand why the series of events have played out the way they have, but it isn't our responsibility to understand. We only have to trust (Proverbs 3:5).

> *Trust in the Lord with all your heart and lean not to your own understanding.*

THE PATH OF LEAST RESISTANCE

Even though God has a distinct purpose to make His kingdom known in your life, the path can be confusing and frustrating. Don't misunderstand me. I am not saying God is confusing but rather the path to His calling can be. God is not and never will be the reason for confusion in your life. If the calling ultimately serves and advances the Kingdom of God, why would God lead you down a path that just confuses you? After all, He did tell us He is not the author of confusion (1 Corinthians 14:33). The path can be confusing because we take our eyes off of the One who the calling serves and end up in a place that we don't recognize.

My grandfather (known to me as Papa) used to tour in a Southern gospel band, and every night after a show, they would all pile in the tour bus and drive to the next show. They didn't have a bus driver, so they took turns driving two hours at a time through the night. One night, Papa's turn came up, and he took a "shortcut" on some weird back road and got super lost. This was before the days of technology telling you where you are at all times. Instead of waking someone else up to help him or even just turning around to retrace his route, he just kept going. He drove through the entire night and finally got back on the right road. When the rest of the band woke up, they asked, "Why are we only 70 miles from the place we played last night?"

Sometimes when we take our eyes off Jesus, we can make a wrong turn or two and get a little lost spiritually. During these times, we tend to carry on without asking anyone to help or even just stopping to retrace our steps. We can spend a long time just driving around trying to find something we recognize. But just because you get back to a place you recognize doesn't mean you're in the correct place. Recognizing your location might mean you're in a familiar, comfortable place. It's just like Papa. Finally finding a road he recognized didn't mean he was any farther down the road than when he took the wrong turn; he just kept driving because that was the easiest thing to do.

I majored in electrical engineering as a college student at the University of Alabama at Birmingham (or, as known to those who attended, UAB). One of the courses required in this major is electrical circuits. In the theory of electrical circuits, current takes the path of least resistance. Often, we do the same. We become flustered with our wrong turns, or failures, and naturally find ourselves taking another path with the least amount of resistance. You still may be moving, but it doesn't mean you're moving in the right direction.

THE FAILURE IN OBEDIENCE

When we walk on the correct path with God, we can definitely feel the resistance of our enemy or our flesh; but know that the resistance you feel doesn't mean that you're failing. Sometimes in our walk, resistance can come from obedience. It sounds like an oxymoron, I know. Think on this character in the Bible, though—Job. This man had what others would define as failures to spare for his life and all of ours. But was Job really a failure? Job had such faith in the Lord that the Bible calls him "blameless and upright" (Job 1:1). Job was blessed and quite wealthy and was "the greatest man" (Job 1:3). This guy was so in touch with God. God Himself told Satan if there was anyone in the earth that won't deny me, it's Job. That's an incredible honor! So in God's sovereignty, Satan attacks Job's possessions, family, and his body. Through all of this, Job was so miserable that he said, "May the day of my birth perish, and the night that said, 'A boy is conceived!'" (Job 3:1). Aaron's translation: I don't want to be alive because the misery I feel is greater than the desire to live.

But in his deepest, darkest miseries, Job stayed strong. His wife even told him to give up and die (Job 2:10). Job simply responded, "Shall we accept good from God, and not trouble?" (Job 2:10). That's true faith! I would like to think I would respond the same way, but I know that if I'm just late to a meeting because I had to stop and get coffee, I start praying, "Lord, just start to work all the bad for my good."

At this point, no one had hope for Job: his best friends thought he'd be better off dead. As we discussed in the beginning of this chapter, the ones around you will highlight your failures in life the most. Isn't it interesting how obedience can look like failure? I believe we chalk up hard and grueling times as failures. You must realize as you walk with Jesus that not everything is always ideal. I'm positive Job didn't think things were chill when his body was covered in boils so bad that his friends cried at the sight of him (Job 2:12). Walking in our God-called purpose requires obedience, but with every act of obedience, there is an act of resistance. Like for every action, there's a reaction. You know, physics and stuff.

There is always resistance because there is always an adversary—Satan. Satan's whole point of afflicting Job was to pull him out of obedience and to stop believing in God. In general, that is Satan's entire tactic for us. He doesn't want you to walk with Jesus. He doesn't want you to experience peace. Satan doesn't want you to fulfill the purpose God has instilled inside your core because he understands that God's purpose will advance the Kingdom of Heaven. We will have trials. Jesus even says, "In this world you will have trouble. But take heart! I have overcome the world." (John 16:33). How can we fail if we are already victorious through Christ?

When our lives are faced with resistance, we immediately feel a failing and a fearful sensation like we are not going to get through this moment. Our natural instinct is to give up. If it isn't going to end well, just stop before you get to the end. That way, we avoided failure, right? Sometimes, even your best friends will mourn you and consider you foolish for persevering. This perseverance is obedience. God doesn't quit on His promises, and He doesn't make mistakes. He is sovereign, and we must be obedient in His sovereignty. He is removing what is in our lives to establish something much better (Hebrews 10:9).

But in the middle of the trial, it can be a fearful thing to be obedient. It's like the scene in *Indiana Jones and the Last Crusade* where Indiana must step off the ledge onto a hidden path.[24] He can't see it because the path is camouflaged by the bottom of the pit. The next step of obedience is often hidden by the fear of what happens if the next step ends in failure. In other words, our obedience is hindered by the fear of failure. Indiana Jones has gone through the gauntlet just to get to the beginning of the last obstacle. Only one obstacle remains before he reaches what he is searching for. It appears that the path has run out and his next step could end in failure (i.e., death). Indiana was afraid and rightly so given that the next step could kill him, and honestly, against his better judgment, takes a step only to find the path. After he takes the step and the path is revealed, it makes total sense, and you realize that it was the best decision he could have made. However, during the action of taking the step, the obedience to trust that there will be a path seems like a failure. In the same sense, Job's decision to be obedient in trusting the sovereignty of God even in the part of his life that felt the most insecure and tumultuous seemed like failure. His body, soul, and spirit were broken. His family was killed. His provisions were stripped away. But despite all Job's disparity, he remained obedient. Obedience is simply eschewing temporal desires and pleasures to make way for something greater and everlasting to work in your life.

Obedience is not easy and can sometimes feel like death. So, why do we obey? Why do we yield to God and not our pleasures? Romans 5:3–4 says,

> *We also glory in our sufferings, because we know that suffering produces perseverance; perseverance, character; and character, hope.*

The failures or sufferings we face at the end of it all produce the hope we desire. But the obedience we live in during the middle produces the perseverance we need to reach that hope.

TOO PERFECT TO FAIL

This whole path thing can be frustrating. Failure, obedience, and your natural state of wanting to give up can cause some frustration. This is totally understandable. Even though we are walking in what God created us to be, we are still humans. But if we sulk and operate in frustration, we will become perfectionists.

Kids who participate in athletics or scholastics are taught that perfectionism is the key to placing you at the top of the food chain. We are taught that if we focus on the minute details that no one else pays attention to, we will be primed for more opportunities than others. While this is true, perfectionism can have a dark side. Our human minds tend to think with this same structure in every aspect of our lives. If we are procrastinators with schoolwork, we likely procrastinate with house projects. Likewise, if we are perfectionists with small cleaning projects around the house, we are likely perfectionists elsewhere. Don't misunderstand; perfectionism has its place, but there must be a balance. It's the same with procrastination. Sometimes it can be a good thing to let tasks go to the wayside and realize the most important battle to win is your sanity. If the project can wait, sometimes it's all right to let it wait. Don't worry. It'll be there for you later, I promise. Other times, it's important to be a perfectionist. I'm sure your employer is grateful you do your job with a spirit of perfection. But few actually live in balance, while most carry a spirit of perfectionism with them wherever they go: to their jobs, to their children, to their marriages, and even to God. These perfections may seem small and insignificant, but they get heavy over time and wear you down.

Think of it this way: if you pick up a five-pound weight and begin taking it with you everywhere you go, eventually, you are going to start noticing there is something heavier about you. Carrying around perfection works the same way. You may not notice it at first, and some people may have a different type of strength than others and can carry it longer; but eventually, everyone will notice the effects of carrying this weight. The weight of perfection is heavy and unrelenting. This weight is dangerous to carry, especially into our relationship with God, because He operates in the opposite of perfectionism—grace.

Don't tense up on me. I am not saying God is not perfect. He is completely perfect in His ways (Psalm 18:30). However, perfectionism is different. Perfectionism is based entirely on your performance. It's like a mirror that points out only your flaws. Perfectionism will never allow you to progress because it will keep you focused on the things in your life you can't make right. It makes you look inwardly to know you're good enough.

Grace is different. Grace will allow continuous progression because you look to Jesus for approval of yourself instead of a mirror that is manipulated to make you think you are less than who you are in Christ. Grace is so far beyond our human mindset that few people actually walk in it. Grace is tender and kind. Perfection is jagged and brutal. Grace desires to build you and make you stronger. Perfection seeks only to point out the flaws and mistakes, all to make you "better." They are opposites.

As humans, we naturally have flaws that God has to work out of us, and I don't know anyone who actually enjoys being told they are wrong. Naturally, it can become difficult to receive correction. Our human nature wants to put an end to the things that are uncomfortable, so, if we are growing weary of correction, it is natural to find whatever way necessary to end the correcting. Enter perfection. If we're perfect, there's no need to correct us, right? I mean, the logic checks out. The next time we feel a correction from the Holy Spirit, we cloak ourselves with a spirit of perfection to focus on how never to make the mistake again. In short, perfectionism is a strategy to avoid failure. However, this instantaneously becomes a slippery slope.

I can give testimony to this. My confession to you: I am an insane perfectionist. You know that roommate who is so detailed that he or she wants you to put something back right after you use it? Yep, that's me. While this can be good for having a clean and orderly house, it can cause pain. If there is a project my wife wants done and I'm not sure how to complete it, I simply procrastinate. I don't procrastinate out of laziness; I procrastinate because I haven't ironed out every detail of how I'm going to complete the project. My perfectionism makes me feel as if I'm too lowly of a mind to figure it out. So you see, this desire to be perfect can actually backfire and produce results opposite to what we intended. The intentions are pure, but the struggle for self-perfection causes us to hinder the lesson God wants us to learn. We try to be so perfect that we become unteachable. If I would just start a new project, I would learn a new skill while completing the project. Instead, projects are pushed off because I would rather be perfect in something I already know than face a project in which I could fail.

In our search for perfection, the focus shifts off God's plan and toward the selfish desire to be perfect. But remember, our goal isn't to be perfect; it is only to keep growing in grace. This shift of focus, in turn, causes us to fight God in what He is trying to teach us. We stop listening to the teaching words He is speaking to develop and grow us so that we are better equipped to walk in our purpose. Instead, we become frustrated and jaded toward God because we don't believe He is satisfied with our performance. The spirit of perfectionism removes us from a grace-filled life into a performance-based life. A performance-based mindset cannot exist in a growing relationship with God. The relationship becomes a task-oriented "judge-prisoner" relationship in which God is the hammer-slamming judge. We just hope the Judge becomes pleased with our efforts enough to let us into the Kingdom with good behavior. When we become so focused on perfectly executing the correct moves, our perception of God skews who He really is. But doesn't God know that we're human? Doesn't His Word say we are but dust? (Genesis 2:7).

> *Then the Lord God formed man from the dust of the ground and breathed into his nostrils the breath of life, and the man became a living being.*

In Isaiah 45:12, God says, "It is I who made the earth and created mankind upon it." Why would God create us from dust, declare it is He who created us, and then look for every opportunity to punish us? If God was expecting us to be perfect, Jesus would have never stepped foot on this earth. The expectation of perfection is not placed on our shoulders but on Jesus's (Romans 8:3).

> *For what the Law was powerless to do because it was weakened by the flesh, God did by sending his own Son in the likeness of sinful flesh to be a sin offering.*

When we attempt to remove the responsibility of perfection from Jesus and place it on ourselves, our inner fear and anxiety take over the operation. Our intentions come out of a good place—to prove that we understand the lesson God is teaching us and that we will never again repeat the same mistake. However, this intention leads to operating directly against what He intended. God intended grace to be given by

His Son's punishment, but we inflict the punishment upon ourselves in the name of perfection. This is the direct opposite of what God wants for our lives, but we convince ourselves God is pleased when we self-inflict pain and punishment. So we dig deeper into perfection despite this weight never being intended for us to carry. Humans cannot be perfect. You will never be perfect. There is a gap between us and Holy God that purposefully requires grace and the perfection of Jesus.

Perfectionism is thought to be an antonym and the cure for failure but can instead hinder our growth of becoming who God has called us to be. Perfectionism makes us become angry at the fact we aren't good enough and cause us to take a path of least resistance where we are good enough. Ironically, perfectionism can actually move us off of the path God has called us to be on. Perfectionism always seems to operate out of a place of good intention, but the intentions are instead selfish. It takes the focus off of the big picture God has laid out and places it on how we performed in a momentary task. We get so caught up in the thought of avoiding failure that we can become fixated on perfecting every move we make. It's globally known that if we desire perfectionism, we will be the best; that's what makes us champions. And yes, to some degree that's true. Attention to detail and dedication are desirable qualities that should be sought after. However, there is a difference in detail and scrutiny and a difference in dedication and worry. The spirit of perfectionism can take what started in a good place and make it into a dark, shameful, a mentally draining place. Here's the honest truth that no one who lives in a spirit of perfection wants to hear: you are going to fail every day. How do I know every day? You're a human, and as long as you're on this earth, you will always be a human. How silly is it to expect perfection from something that, at its core, is imperfect?

WHEN FAILURE LOOKS LIKE GRACE

So how do you get out of this draining place of perfection and live in renewing grace? It isn't easy, and it is a choice you are going to have to make every morning. That being said, here's where we are going to start: take all the moments you failed and when felt you weren't perfect, and lay them before God. You know all those nightmare moments that arise in your mind over and over again randomly and haunt you? Take those, every single one, and place them before God. Uncover every mistake, and don't hold anything back. What's your mindset? Are you scared? Are you nervous? You're nervous because you're vulnerable, and you think that since God can see your mistakes, you now have to pay the consequences. Thankfully, there is no punishment for your imperfections! There is no punishment because Jesus already accepted the punishment upon himself. He removed all the imperfections from your life through a moment of perfect sacrifice (1 John 3:5).

> *But you know that he appeared so that he might take away our sins. And in him is no sin.*

God the Father sees you. He sees you through the lens of this beating, the blood-stained cross, through the power of the crown of thorns and through the imperfection that was bestowed on Jesus through the nails in His hands (Colossians 2:13–14).

> *When you were dead in your sins and in the uncircumcision of your flesh, God made you alive with Christ. He forgave us all our sins, having canceled the charge of our legal indebtedness, which stood against us and condemned us; he has taken it away, nailing it to the cross.*

This is the perfectionism God sees you through. Our failures cannot be avoided, but they aren't supposed to be. Christ took responsibility for all of our failures and imperfections, and in that, we can take comfort that as we fail, God doesn't look at us and see the failure. God sees us as perfect through the Grace of His Son, Jesus.

PATIENCE ON THE PATH

IN YOUR PATIENCE ...

The path of God's purpose is based on one thing in everyone's life—a promise. I don't know exactly what God has promised you for your life—or even just for this season—but I know there is a promise. It would be lovely if God promised the purpose, the purpose happened, and we could simply move on to the next promise. I wish it were that simple. The promises God makes could take some time to develop and take form. His process then forces us to do what we all hate—waiting. Waiting is hated because it produces patience, and patience is uncomfortable.

"In your patience, possess ye your soul" (Luke 21:19 KJV). "This too shall pass" (my grandmother). One of these quotes is holy and biblical. Both were quoted by my grandmother 192,837,645 times in my life. She quoted them to give me hope like the Lord lays out in Jeremiah. They did not.

When I was eighteen, I had a lateral meniscal transplant (in other words, the cushy stuff in my knee went janky, and I needed another slapped in). The typical rehab time for this kind of surgery is around eight months, and in my experience, I wasn't walking right for a year. About a week in, I'm sitting on the toilet sick as a dog, high on medications, and haven't even felt my leg since I went under for surgery. For some of you, this was just college. About that time, my grandmother calls me to say, "I know this is trying, but remember, in your patience possess ye your soul. This too shall pass." Oh! Thank you! All better now! She telling me that my soul would be formed by the patience I had did not make the physical therapy appointments feel any better. Nor did it make my leg get stronger. She quoting that only made me angry!

I know you're thinking, *What a sweet lady! She called you up to give you encouragement in a time of need. How dare you get angry with her!* You have to understand my frustration. All these "encouraging quotes" were coming from the same lady that said, "Lord, teach me patience and teach it to me now." She obviously knew the importance of patience but also had a human element of dissatisfaction that we all share.

The discomfort and dissatisfaction come when our questions aren't immediately answered and we are forced to exercise patience in our lives. Patience is derived from a Latin word meaning "suffering." I know that sentence doesn't sound like a good sales pitch to make you buy into being patient; however, when this discomfort and suffering comes, be glad! I know it sounds like I'm still high off medication trying to tell you to be glad about suffering, but be glad, because "suffering produces perseverance; perseverance, character; and character; hope" (Romans 5:4). The hope that is developed by the process of discomfort is the reason we can trust in God with our paths we walk down. So we have to be patient *for* our purpose.

Pastor John Gray (pastor of Relentless Church) said, "Jesus underwent thirty years of preparation for three years of ministry and three hours of purpose." You have to be prepared to enter into your purpose when the time comes. How do we prepare? The Word prepared comes from the Latin word *praeparare*. This Latin word can be broken down into two separate words: *prae* (meaning "before") and *parare* (meaning "make ready").[22] God wants to make you ready before the time comes to display your purpose. We just have to be patient.

LET GO AND BE WEAK

I believe the key to patience during our purpose is in Psalm 46:10, which says, "Be still and know that I am God." If I were to tell my six-year-old nephew to be still, his response (if he felt like obeying) would be to quiet himself so as not to make a sound. This verse, however, doesn't exactly have the meaning we would think in our language. The author, King David, didn't speak English. He was the King of Israel; whose language is Hebrew. The Hebrew root of still comes from *rapha*, which translates to, "meaning to be weak, to let go, to release."[7] When God spoke this verse, He wasn't asking us to be still. He was giving a commandment of stillness.

This same word is seen in Exodus 14:13–14:

> Moses answered the people, "Do not be afraid. Stand firm, and you will see the deliverance the Lord will bring you today. The Egyptians you see today will never see you again. The Lord will fight for you; you need only be still."

If you stop and evaluate what was happening around this verse, it's almost impossible to think being still was even an option. The Israelites were up against death—the end of their path—or so they thought. Israel was called to be God's chosen people, but place yourself up against an ocean with an army of six hundred chariots coming toward you and see if you feel called. Oh, and let's not forget that the Lord told the Israelites to go to this specific place (Exodus 14:2).

> Tell the Israelites to turn back and encamp near Pi Hahiroth, between Migdol and the sea. They are to encamp by the sea.

Here we have God's called people following His instruction with what seems to be two choices: (1) Attempt to swim away from the army and probably drown, or (2) get slaughtered by a gigantic army. I don't know how everything in your life has played out, but I'm guessing you've been at this crossroad before. Feeling like there is no escape: from your finances, your job, your boss, or your shame. There doesn't seem to be much purpose to the path at this point. But what if I told you all you had to do was be still? What if I told you all you had to do to be released from your oppression was to become weak? Up against death, God tells the children of Israel to be weak.

> *Why are you crying out to me? Tell the Israelites to move on. Raise your staff and stretch out your hand over the sea to divide the water so that the Israelites can go through the sea on dry ground." (Exodus 14: 15–16).*

I love how God so nonchalantly tells his people to quit being so dramatic over a "simple thing" like death and move on. But when I read these verses altogether, I can't help but wonder why God would say to "be still" and then give a command to "raise your staff"? Isn't that the opposite of each other? I believe the verses are showing us that sometimes, we have to use what God has equipped us with at that time to move forward—not because what we alone possess is enough but because of what God can do with what we possess. God can use what we have to make a way, even if it is us just being still.

BACK FROM THE PAST

If we continue to read Exodus 14, the Lord says, "I will gain glory through Pharaoh and all his army, through his chariots and his horsemen" (Exodus 14:17). God is telling us His Kingdom is going to be exalted through the very thing that is coming to destroy Israel.

My dad wrote this song when I was a kid. This was pre-Hillsong, Elevation, and Highlands worship. He wrote a song that sang, "If I know You, You'll take what Satan meant to bring me down and turn it into a robe and crown, if I know You." The very thing that stares Israel in the face, what they've been bound by and held captive by, is coming back into their lives. It's coming back with a vengeance. Their previous captor aims not to enslave them again but to obliterate them. Maybe you can relate. Maybe you became free of watching lustful things, but now without you even realizing what happened, it's slipped back in, and you're trapped—even more than you ever have been before. Perhaps you looked to God after an affair that caused a broken marriage, and God heard you. God placed your marriage together again. But now you can't come home immediately after work. You have to go by the gym to shower because you don't smell like your wife's perfume. Maybe there are mental thoughts you became free from and now all you can feel is the heaviness you thought you'd never face again. The bondage you're delivered from always comes back with intentions to kill and destroy. Notice, I said *delivered from* and not *escaped from*. You didn't slip out the back door of sin's prison cell. God heard your cry and busted open the whole prison (Acts 16:25–26). However, death doesn't take defeat well. Oppression looks to reenter your life to kill and destroy. Your sin longs to defeat you.

In the midst of Egypt seeking Israel's demise, God says His good will be done. He is saying that the very thing trying to take you captive again coming back into the lives of His children is going to be used for His glory. As Moses stretched out his hand, the water parted, allowing Israel to walk through on dry land untouched and unharmed. But Egypt chased after them. Israel was walking toward the next place in the path of their purpose, and the only thing that could hinder them was what was behind them—their past. Israel would have been captured too if they had filled their hearts with fear of their recent captor rather than stilling their hearts in God. But they walked in stillness; they became weak and knew that this situation would lift up the name of God. As their past came upon them, God caused the chariots of the Egyptians to malfunction and cause them to exist no more (Exodus 14:28).

If you still your heart and become patient in your spirit during fearful, difficult times, the Lord will not only bring you to the place you need to be but also completely destroy that which has burdened, enslaved, and pursued you.

If you notice in the passage, "in the last watch of night," the Lord caused a confusing malfunction in the Egyptian army (Exodus 14:24). The passage goes on to say that, "at daybreak," the sea rolled back over the Egyptian army. I don't believe the time of day these events occurred was a coincidence. Just as in our own lives, when all hope seems lost, our purpose seems not to exist and darkness surrounds. Then the Lord intervenes. As God takes action in our lives, the darkness begins to fade as daylight breaks through. That daylight erases the past; it's a new day! You aren't held captive by what has kept you from living in your purpose. That captor can no longer chase you! You are free to walk in hope and peace to fulfill the calling God has placed on your life specifically.

Some of us, though, feel as if the dusk overshadowing our lives has been glooming around for too long. We just can't seem to find that daybreak, no matter how we pray or how we believe. But no matter how long we've been waiting, there is one thing that could give hope in the darkest times in life, and that is the promises of God. When God speaks, there is no maybe. What He speaks will come to pass. We sometimes need to have patient faith until His promises become our reality.

Abram knew God called him to father generations, but there was one slight problem: he wasn't a father. I would be stoked for God to call on me and say, "Hey, man. So yeah, I'm gonna create the generations kind of after you. Oh yeah, one more thing. You're going to, like, start the family tree of My Son. No pressure, bro." That's a pretty heavy purpose in life. Now, let's place ourselves in Abram's sandals for a bit. You've left your home, the only home you've ever known, and God has you traveling to a place that He "will show you" (Genesis 12:1).

> *The Lord had said to Abram, "Go from your country, your people and your father's household to the land I will show you."*

You have no place yet. Just a promise from God: "To your offspring I will give this land" (Genesis 12:7). So you ponder about God's promise as you pitch a tent to sleep that night. (Really. He slept in a tent the same night God spoke to him about his offspring inheriting the land). You've become a vagabond with a promise that your home will stretch to "all the land that you see" (Genesis 13:15).

Let's now move further away from the present and slip on another pair of sandals—Noah's. God has spoken to you. He has called you to fulfill a purpose because you are the only blameless man among your time (I'd be feeling pretty good about myself if that were me—just saying). The purpose God is calling you to is to establish righteous life again on the earth after He destroys it. That's a pretty sweet gig. The righteousness God sees in you is enough to make Him call you by name and do His will when no one else will. Only one hindrance: God is calling you to build a cruise ship for a flood that isn't exactly being projected by the local weatherman. As in, it's supposed to be sunny and 85°F type of weekend. Anyone ever been there before? You know you've received a Word from God and you are determined to walk it out, so you begin attempts to get to that purpose in your life. With every attempt, you realize there isn't a way to actually get to that point.

Take this for instance, you hear the voice of God come unto you and say, "I will make you a political leader—a senator." Wouldn't that be dumb exciting? You're so stoked, and you change your entire life to focus on getting your life to be a senator, but there's only one problem—you're twelve, and you have to be thirty to run for senator. Does that mean you didn't hear the voice of the Lord? No, not at all! When God truly speaks to you, it is unmistakable. Most of the time, God's purpose begins in tiny portions. Pastor Bruce Terry from Liberty Church in Birmingham said, "The world wants to let you believe that you aren't successful unless you start big. Everything you do must be something large and noticeable, but God's Kingdom works the exact opposite. God will begin a purpose in you as a seed, and grow you in His timing to see if you will be faithful with the small promises before you inherit the large promises" (author's paraphrase). It takes patience to fully inherit a promise of God. When a seed is planted, it takes time for it to grow and develop. But trust me when I say God doesn't grow any small promises. God has simply planted a seed the size of a mustard seed in your heart, and that mustard seed is going to take a whole summer of nurturing before harvest time. So will some promises turn into such large purposes that the planted seed needs time to be nurtured and grow. That purpose put on your life may require unhealthy things to be weeded out. Maybe the way to truly walk in your God-calling is by addressing the roadblocks obstructing your path. It could be bitterness, it could be pride, or maybe it could be impatience.

God will only introduce a promise into your life when it's time to begin your growth. If the promise seems so far away, be patient. Be patient because He is doing a work in you. Be patient because He's transforming you. Be patient and trust that God will lead you to the place where His promise will be fulfilled.

FOUNDATION OF THE PATH

THE CHASM AND THE BRIDGE

If you're anything like me, you may learn well by examples: so let's take a deeper look at some biblical figures we've already gained some wisdom from. Abraham received a promise from God, walked in that purpose placed on his life, and became the man that birthed nations. Noah obeyed God and became responsible for re-birthing the earth. Moses was called to convince a powerful leader to release a people that had been enslaved for hundreds of years. How did these men get to a place in their lives where they walked in a fulfilled, God-destined purpose? In all three cases, there is a promise made with no real evidence that the promise was naturally realistic. Abraham was an old man with no son; yet he was supposed to be the father of many. Noah was to build a boat to save his family and all the creatures of the earth so that repopulation could occur after God destroyed the earth by a flood, but the ground wasn't even wet. Moses was to march back into the same place he ran away from to persuade a ruler who clearly wasn't a believer that God commands his slaves must be set free, yet he had a speech impediment.

So, what makes this God-spoken word become a reality? There is a natural chasm between the promise God has made and the place we are in our lives. If there wasn't a chasm, then God's word wouldn't be a promise because it would be a reality. Therefore, to obtain the spoken promise, we need to cross the chasm. We must build a bridge to cross this chasm. A bridge that takes us from where we are to the promised place. Abraham couldn't be the father of many if he never left the house of his father. Noah wouldn't have been prepared to survive the flood if the ark was never built. Moses may not have been able to free the Israelites if he wasn't first free of Egypt himself. The promise of God can't be delivered until a bridge covers the chasm. The bridge will allow a solid foundation to support you and whoever journeys with you to the promise God has in store for your life.

The question lingers—how do you build this bridge? Building a bridge isn't easy, and every bridge must be made structurally sound to withstand the forces of nature. It takes months, sometimes years, of meetings to construct detailed processes and produce drawings approved by engineers before the first stone is even laid.

There is a specific bridge design that I find absolutely fascinating—the arch bridge. This design is actually the oldest type of bridge design and became quite popular in the days of the Roman Empire. I find these types of bridges interesting because of the method that is used during construction called centering. This method allows the arch bridge to be built from both sides at the same time; the centering method supports both sides of the bridge until the bridge is connected at the top.[8] The bridge is completely unstable until the two sides connect and lock in place together in the middle.

The importance of the type of design that arch bridges offer is the curved design of the bridge. The curved design doesn't push forces straight down when a load is applied to the top of it (e.g., when a truck is driven over it), but rather, the forces are pushed along the arch curve until the load is absorbed by the arch supports on each end.

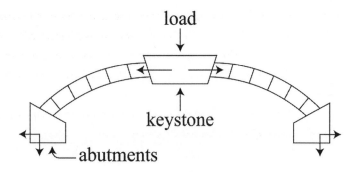

A bridge with load applied.

The supports of the bridge, which are called abutments, have the responsibility of maintaining the stability of the bridge. While the abutments maintain the stability, the forces applied to the bridge are conveyed by a central keystone (the keystone is the largest brick in the top center of the above image). This keystone is on top of the arch and distributes the forces to the rocks adjacent to the keystone down and outward, which creates a rigid and strong structure to the bridge.[10] The keystone holds the integrity of the bridge. Without the keystone, there is no bridge because the keystone is the capstone. The keystone in the middle of the bridge bears the weight of the rest of the bridge. The more force applied to the bridge, the stronger the structure becomes.[11]

This bridge construction that has two free-standing sides is important. Let one free-standing side represent God and the other side of the bridge represent you. The two separated ends represent a natural chasm between us and God that is caused by the natural-born sin inside us. To connect to a Holy God and walk into His designed purpose, there has to be a meeting of God and man. The good news is that this meeting has already taken place—when Jesus was born. Jesus came to this earth, was crushed for our sins, and now sits at the right hand of the Father. God's side of the bridge already existed. It then remains that our side must be constructed. It wouldn't be smart to begin construction on our half of the bridge arbitrarily. Our half of the bridge must be centered with God's constructed half. Just as an arch bridge undergoes a centering method, our hearts have to become centered to Jesus, who is the keystone. Centering our hearts with the heart of Jesus as well as trusting His truth is what locks our hearts in place with the heart of the Father and constructs a firm, immovable, and unshakeable foundation.

Just as the Bible points out in Hebrews, it is essential that the bridge be constructed out of faith and trust (Hebrews 11:1).

> *Now faith is confidence in what we hope for and assurance about what we do not see.*

This faith bridge takes us from what we don't know confidently into what God knows. Understand, though, that this bridge isn't one being built out of endless works. God isn't waiting on us to do enough spiritual chores so he can grant us our allowance of purpose; but construction progresses when we do intentional faith-filled actions that His voice leads us to do in faith of His promise. The Message paraphrases Hebrews 11:1–2 this way:

> *The fundamental fact of faith of existence is that this trust in God, this faith, is the firm foundation under everything that makes this life worth living. It's our handle on what we can't see. The act of faith is what distinguished our ancestors, set them above the crowd. (The Message)*

Building a faith bridge allows us to stand firmly on God's promise without anxiety; without the stress of the unknown. Faith provides a structure that is sound and solid, that will not fault under heavy winds or crushing waves. If what your faith is built on is structurally sound, there is no storm that could shake you. When the storms do come into our lives (not *if* but *when*), you don't have to have the storm calmed before you can walk through it. You won't have to wait until the storm calms because Jesus, the foundation on which you walk, is the calm.

When the waves tower and hurricanes try to destroy your life, you don't have to be afraid. The forces that the storms bring won't be placed only on you but also on your foundation. If your foundation is strong, the forces won't break you. Just like the keystone in the arch bridge, the more the force, the stronger Jesus is.

Your foundation is built on Jesus, so whatever storm is raging against you cannot harm you. Psalm 91:9–10 states,

> If you say "The Lord is my refuge." And you make the Most High your dwelling, no harm will overtake you, no disaster will come near your tent.

A LONG-LASTING STRUCTURE

The arch bridge design became so popular in the days of the Roman Empire because the structure enabled bridge builders to arch the bridge much higher while lowering the mass of the entire structure. Due to this design, the constructed bridges were empowered to withstand the pressures and strains of inclement weather conditions, which could include floods or strong rivers.[10] The Roman Empire used the design of the arch bridge to construct astounding bridges; as time went on, medieval and renaissance architects enhanced the designs that the Romans had lain in place. The latter generations of architects created arch bridges with more narrow piers and increased the spans of the arches. They also improved upon the initial design of the Romans to construct some of the most extravagant and wondrous bridges known to man's eye.[10] I point this out because as you construct your bridge by working in functional, active faith, the path you're laying a foundation for might not be initially apparent. The generations that come after you may use the same foundation you've lain to fulfill their God-called purpose.

An interesting aspect of arch bridges is that they were constructed so elements (whether it's water from a river or even people in a city) could pass under the bridges while other traffic could cross above. The bridge you construct may not be just to reach your purpose, but it can also provide multiple paths for future generations to walk down that you may never see in your lifetime. But if you aren't faithful and don't construct the bridge with the keystone holding all the weight, your bridge will lose its integrity and collapse on itself. This collapse could cause harm to yourself, but almost more importantly, the destruction of your bridge could hinder future generations from walking into their promised land. So you may not only be setting up your path, but also the future generation's path; neither will be built unless you construct the bridge to take you where God has purposed you.

To give an example out of my own life, I struggle with self-esteem issues. I don't know where this came from; it has just always been there. I didn't ask for it, and I sure never loved it growing up. It was extremely difficult to live in the mindset of never having confidence in myself when everyone around seemed to have no issues. I remember it being such a crippling fear in my life that when I would play basketball in high school, I became afraid to even shoot the ball because I was terrified of what would happen if I missed. As I grew up, though, I saw this same mental behavior in my dad. After discussing this with him, I realized his father struggled with the same issue. More than likely, so did his father. One day, I was driving home, and I began to discuss with my dad the hardships of the day, which focused mainly on what people thought and said about me—about how lower I felt than anyone else. My dad stopped and said, "Aaron, we're making a pact. This second. We will remove this generational burden that our family has been manipulated into carrying for so long." He was entirely correct. If my father and I don't build the correct foundation to cross this chasm of fear, my children will inherit the same mentality. Why has our family dealt with this crippling fear for so long? To quote a wise old Church Lady of *Saturday Night Live*, "Satan, hm?"[23] Satan hates when generations are established because that means a path is being built to link us directly to God's heart. So Satan attempts to make this path crumble any way that he can so the foundation is never laid. However, Satan is resourceful. He's cyclical. If one thing tripped your grandfather up and it was never dealt with, you better believe he is going to bring the same opposition at you. The point here is that a foundation must be laid, not just for our own purpose but for the future generations to be launched forward. Just think, where would the nation of Israel have been if Abraham didn't lay the foundation that he did in God's purpose?

WHEN THE BRIDGE ISN'T BUILT

Saul was anointed King over Israel; he was transported from a lowly place to the highest level of importance one could have in a nation. In those days, Israel's faith in God and His power had diminished, and they desired something more tangible (1 Samuel 8:20).

> *Then we will be able to be like other nations, with a king to lead us and to go out before us and fight our battles.*

Israel desired to have a King to go before them so they would have a "king to lead" them to be like the other nations. Even though Israel's desire was based on a lack of faith in God, God honored the desires of Israel's heart, and through Samuel, He appointed a king over Israel. Saul was out of the tribe of Benjamin, which was the smallest tribe of Israel. Also, the clan Saul belonged to was the least of all clans of the tribe of Benjamin (1 Samuel 9:21). Saul was humbled to be appointed king over Israel. As time went forward in Saul's kingship, the focus shifted from the humility of becoming king to the power of being king. In 1 Samuel 13, the Philistines gathered to battle Israel. The Philistine's numbers were significantly greater than the Israelite army. The Israelite soldiers feared for their lives and began to run away and hide from the Philistines. Saul waited seven days for Samuel to show up as Samuel had instructed because it was a promise Samuel would make sacrifices to God on behalf of the nation of Israel (1 Samuel 10:8). On the seventh day, Saul grew impatient and made the sacrifice himself to "better" the opportunities of winning the battle with the Philistines. As soon as the sacrifice was made, Samuel becomes enraged that Saul had done the exact opposite of what God instructed. In the time of uncertainty, Saul looked within himself for the answer to the situation rather than waiting on the promise of God. For this, Samuel said to Saul,

> *Now your kingdom will not endure; the Lord has sought out a man after his own heart and appointed him ruler of his people, because you have not kept the Lord's command. (1 Samuel 13:14).*

In 1 Samuel 15, the Lord commanded Saul to take out the Amalekites completely, but Saul took the king of the Amalekites alive and kept the best of their sheep and cattle. Once again, as Saul leaned more on his own understanding, the Lord said to Samuel,

> *I regret that I have made Saul king, because he has turned away from me and has not carried out my instructions. (1 Samuel 15:11)*

When Samuel confronted Saul about his errors, Saul responded, "I was afraid of the men and so I gave into them" (1 Samuel 15:24). In turn, Samuel said to Saul, "The Lord has torn the kingdom of Israel from you today and has given it to one of our neighbors—to one better than you" (1 Samuel 15:28). This grieves Saul's heart, but for the wrong reasons. He pleads with Samuel, "I have sinned. But please honor me before the elders of my people and before Israel" (1 Samuel 15:30). The response of Saul is a confession of guilt and wrongdoing; however, his reason for repentance is not pure. Saul repents so that his power would be restored instead of repenting to understand the heart of the Father.

Saul becomes even more obsessed with the throne itself rather than the God that put him there. This is just where the root of Saul's self-obsession takes place. Since Saul sought after the fulfillment of power to satisfy him instead of the spirit of God, God's spirit had no room to work in Saul's life. This left Saul with an endless void. God rejected Saul as king because Saul refused to walk in the spirit of God;

rather, Saul chose to walk in the spirit of himself. In 1 Samuel 16:14, the Word states,

> *Now the Spirit of the Lord had departed from Saul, and an evil spirit from the Lord tormented him.*

An evil spirit of the Lord? God isn't evil, right? Or does this passage prove that God indeed does have evil in Him? No, a resounding no, is the answer. God is not evil in any way. God is holy, loving, and merciful. I believe that through Saul's perseverance in fulfilling self-empowerment, he ultimately knew he wasn't operating in the same anointing that Samuel had poured over his head. Saul's desires and the spirit of God are fighting. While Saul chose to reject the anointing of God, God still loved Saul. You know that Saul could sense the pulling between what he desired and the purpose God had called him to. Through all of his acts of selfishness, Saul had fits of a "tormenting" spirit (1 Samuel 16:15). Saul felt the pull of God in his heart, and his refusal to change made him begin to go crazy. Like many of us on our path with God, Saul knew what he was supposed to surrender and allow God to do in his life. But his refusal to repent caused a constant war in Saul's mind because the love of the Holy Spirit continuously chased him.

The attendants of Saul decided that when Saul's crazy spells came about, a nice lyre player would be good to have on call. Quick in-depth history lesson, a lyre is a baby harp–looking instrument. When Saul would pitch a fit, the lyre player would play, helping Saul focus his mind on the instrument instead of his torment. So, on Saul's request, a young kid named David was summoned to the same kingdom that he would one day take over from Saul (1 Samuel 16:19). As David enters the kingdom and the service of Saul, the whole Goliath incident goes down, and people start chanting,

> *Saul has slain his thousands and David his tens of thousands. (1 Samuel 18:7)*

In other words, Saul is aight, but David is ten times better. Just after the crowd's chanting, Saul is in his house while David's playing his lyre to make sure Saul is all calm (they didn't have anxiety pills back then, so a curly-headed dude sitting in the corner with a small harp was the best medicine you got), and next thing you know, Saul pretty much loses his mind and chunks a spear at David saying, "I'll pin David to the wall" (1 Samuel 18:11). In case you are not good with social cues, allow me to clear this moment up for you. This is not cool on Saul's part. Never is it acceptable to throw a spear at someone's head when they are helping you. Saul's heart and mind had become so corrupt that he not only completely destroyed the foundation of his path, but he wanted to destroy the foundation of his successor. Before you judge Saul, understand that this isn't uncommon. While we may not throw actual spears at the heads of those who are to succeed us, many times, the preceding generation feels the same conflict that Saul felt because they fail to listen to the voice of God. When the time comes that the preceding generation is to be succeeded, they feel the conviction that they have not laid the foundation necessary to advance the succeeding generation. In light of understanding what they have not completed, Satan finds a window to turn the conviction into condemnation. The lie convinces the preceding generation that their entire walk has been a mistake and God is bringing another along to finally accomplish the job that they could never do. Condemnation then turns into bitterness toward the succeeding generation. Out of the bitterness, a desire is born to do everything in their power to retain their "position" in God's will, wrapping their identity of who they are in the *calling* rather than the *One* who actually called them. The surest way to retain their position is to destroy the foundation of the one who is to succeed them. This is a common scheme of Satan between generations. Using the ingredients of guilt, shame, and bitterness, Satan builds a wall of selfish division between generations that has caused the Church to continuously fight the same battles. Generation after generation, we never actually build a foundation to the Father's heart that will elevate the succeeding generation.

Saul walked in the purpose God had for him, but he refused to walk in the anointing God poured over him. He accepted the kingship that the Lord called him to. He never ran from that calling; however, Saul operated out of *himself* and the desires of his heart instead of the desires of God's heart. That is why God called a complete opposite of Saul to remove him. David was not head and shoulders above the rest like Saul; when Samuel visited the house of Jesse (David's father) to find Saul's replacement, the Lord spoke and said,

> *Do not consider his appearance or his height, for I have rejected him. The Lord does not look at the things people look at. People look at the outward appearance, but the Lord looks at the heart. (1 Samuel 16:7)*

That is why David was anointed to be king—his heart. God doesn't need someone who's tall enough, smart enough, or strong enough; God needs someone who will operate in the desires of His heart instead of the desires of their own. God needs the one who is available to sway with the river of the Spirit. At the end of Saul, Samuel's voice came to him, saying,

> *Because you did not obey the Lord or carry out his fierce wrath against the Amalekites, the Lord will deliver both Israel and you into the hands of the Philistines, and tomorrow you and your sons will be with me. (1 Samuel 28:19)*

Because of Saul's self-righteous kingship, he and his sons were all killed, removing their name from the royal family of Israel (1 Samuel 31:2–4). Saul's self-obsession destroyed the foundation for him and his family, leaving David to inherit a kingdom that was broken by the self-righteousness of Saul.

The kingdom of Israel is broken as David inherits the throne. Saul's son, Ish-Bosheth (I did some research, and this name is actually available to anyone who needs a baby name), was king over Israel (2 Samuel 2:9); the house of Saul and the house of David were at war (2 Samuel 3:1). Even in Saul's death, he was still causing problems for David. Perhaps you could relate to this. Your father or mother has passed on, but still, troubles seem to rise up against you in their name. In Saul's refusal to lay the correct foundation for the generations to follow, the nation is now fighting against each other.

It's incredibly easy in life to focus on yourself to try to better your career, or even just try to give your family the best life possible but completely miss your God purpose. I believe it is important to take care of your family in life and in death, but that goes beyond the financial realm. All those things you inherited from your parents that drive your spouse crazy: those are probably the issues you want to pay attention to. Your parents didn't mean to leave you in a bad position, but they had issues too that they inherited, just as their parents before them. However, there can be a difference between you and them. You have the opportunity to end the generational inheritance. Just because your father was short-tempered and got mad at the drop of a hat doesn't mean you have to live with that. Just because your mother faced insecurities that made her worry and miss some of the most important moments in your life doesn't mean you have to miss the moments of your children's lives. Here's the kicker of it all: if you don't deal with the issues that you hate you've inherited from your parents, you'll pass the same issues on to your children. Think about it this way, if Satan has tripped your family up and caused dysfunction for generations, why would he change anything now? If it works, why would he have to fix anything? It's just like calling a defense in a football game. If the offense is confused, why change the game plan? People wonder why they turn out just like their parents and struggle to understand why their children have the same issues with them as they did with their parents. Usually, it's because they haven't dealt with the hurt they inherited from their parents. This cycle will just keep repeating until someone steps up and changes things, until someone realizes this life isn't about them. We are born to advance the ministry Jesus began on this earth. Maybe that means you have the difficult job—you're the one left to build the bridge. This requires your heart to be in tune with the Father's, not with your own. That's why David was appointed king—his heart. David learned from Saul's mistakes and lined his heart up with God's so the generations following him would be set up to advance the Kingdom of God.

WHEN A GENERATION IS SET UP

Even though David inherits a foundation that hasn't been laid, he holds no bitterness toward Saul. This, above all, is the most important obstacle to overcome. It's a simple solution to place the blame on those that came before you and never address the generational issues, but that bitterness will choke generational growth faster than anything. When David learns of Saul's death in 2 Samuel 1, he becomes angered with the Amalekite that took the life of Saul (2 Samuel 1:6–10). He inquires of the young Amalekite, "Why weren't you afraid to lift your hand to destroy the Lord's anointed?" (2 Samuel 1:14). David sent a man to kill the young Amalekite because David recognized Saul as God's anointed and not as the man that attempted to kill him. David even does as much to say, "Saul and Jonathan—in life they were loved and admired" (2 Samuel 1:23). I'm not entirely sure I could give a eulogy and say that the crazy man who threw a spear at my head and attempted to hunt me down to kill me was "loved." David wrote this in a lament, which, in the time, laments were composed for fallen leaders and heroes (2 Samuel 1:17, footnote).[3] Even though Saul wasn't exactly the best leader, David showed respect to God's anointed who walked before him. For us, the ones who walked before may not have listened to the heart of God as they should have, but don't reject what they did teach you. Take what possibly little foundation they did lay, and use it to build a foundation for those who are to come after you. And be careful not to tear down any foundation that was built by the generation before you out of bitterness just to rebuild it.

Early in his kingship, it's evident that David is planning on going about his kingly actions slightly different than Saul. As the Philistines heard the word that David had become king over Israel, they gathered their full forces to search for him (2 Samuel 5:17). As the Philistines searched for King David, they began to spread out along the valley. Instead of taking advantage of the Philistines to make his kingdom better as Saul did, David considered the Lord in the matter (2 Samuel 5:19). When the Lord responded and instructed David to go, David did not hesitate. David, unlike Saul, did what the Lord had commanded (2 Samuel 5:25). Once again, what made David desirable in God's eyes was the heart that David had after God. David's desire was to bring heaven to earth. This is demonstrated as David desired not only to bring the Ark of the Covenant back to Israel but also to build a temple for it to reside (2 Samuel 7:2). David creates an incredible demonstration for us today. I don't believe it's enough just to know of the covenant God made with us through Jesus's crucifixion and resurrection, but rather, we must create ourselves as a temple for the holiness of Jesus to reside so others may know there is holiness within us. Through David's heart, he began to build a bridge that would connect his purpose with God's purpose. So, God recognized David's heart and promised him that even though David would not exactly be the one building the temple, the generations after would construct the house of God (2 Samuel 7:12–13).

> *When your days are over and you rest with your ancestors, I will raise up your offspring to succeed you, your own flesh and blood, and I will establish his kingdom. He is the one who will build a house for my Name, and I will establish the throne of his kingdom forever.*

God promises David that his son, Solomon, would build the temple *and* God would endure his kingdom forever. David didn't just accept this promise and forget it. David did everything in his power to build the foundation so the next generation would not only have a purpose but be prepared for that purpose.

King David led with responsibility and wisdom. He wasn't a perfect man; none of us are. There are going to be moments in our lives where we mess up. We completely drop the ball, so to speak. In 2 Samuel 24, David took a census throughout the tribes of Israel. This seems harmless; and if I'm honest, it seems logical. I mean, I've never been a king, but it seems fair to know how many people you have in your kingdom. However, the Lord's anger burned against Israel in this matter (2 Samuel 24:1). See, God wasn't angry at the action of taking a census, because, in fact, that is a logical action to take. David took the census in the spirit of pride. Just as God looked at David's heart on the day he was anointed king, God was looking at his heart in all his decisions as king. The footnote of 2 Samuel 24:1 states, "The mere taking of a census was hardly sinful, but in this instance, it represented an unwarranted glorying in and dependence upon human power rather than the Lord" (2 Samuel 24:1, footnote)[3]. David wanted to see how large and powerful his kingdom has grown. Sound familiar? (*Cough*, Saul, *cough*.) The Lord's anger burned against all of Israel because this decision was larger than David. The action of taking a census to measure the power of a kingdom demonstrated the same insecurities Israel had when they were too weak and desired a King.

What makes David admirable in this, though, is how he handled his failure. As God's anger struck through Israel, leading to the death of 70,000 people, David called to the Lord,

> *I have sinned; I, the shepherd, have done wrong. These are but sheep. What have they done? Let your hand fall on me and my family.* (2 Samuel 24:15, 17).

Unlike his predecessor, David humbled himself and accepted the responsibility of his mistakes. He reminded himself that he was the leader of the kingdom that would only thrive if his heart was centered with God's. In verse 17, David begins to realign or recenter his heart with God's heart, and through the centering of hearts, the plague of Israel caused by David's action ceased. Once again, David didn't allow the mistakes of his predecessor—in this case, pride—to continue to the next generation. He saw the harm of the pride he inherited and put an end to it. David wasn't just living out his purpose; he was laying a foundation for latter generations.

As David enters old age, he realizes the best way to prepare Solomon for inheriting a kingdom is to teach him what he will need to know. In 1 Chronicles 22, David discloses to Solomon that he is to build the temple of God. If I were Samuel, I'm not sure how exactly I would take this news. That's a heavy purpose to receive. But because David laid the foundation of a solid path, Solomon had all that he would need. David bestowed on Solomon all of the plans and resources he had gathered for building the temple. The plans were so detailed that they had the weight of every item to be constructed (1 Chronicles 28:11–18). Solomon didn't just receive a purpose that day; he received a foundation that had already been laid. Before Solomon becomes king, David prays over Solomon, "May the Lord give you discretion and understanding when he puts you in command over Israel, so that you may keep the law of the Lord your God" (1 Chronicles 22:12). He also prays,

> *Lord, the God of our Fathers ... keep these desires and thoughts in the hearts of your people forever, and keep their hearts loyal to you. And give my son Solomon the wholehearted devotion to keep your commandments, statutes and decrees and to do everything to build the palatial structure for which I have provided. (1 Chronicles 29:18–19)*

First Chronicles captures the last quote of David before he passes away, "Praise the Lord your God" (1 Chronicles 29:20). David ended his life much differently than Saul did. Saul's life ended at the edge of his own blade, while David's life ended at a "good old age, having enjoyed a long life, wealth and honor" (1 Chronicles 29:28). Saul's kingdom fell apart at his own hand because of his self-obsession, which removed his entire family from the purpose of Israel. David's kingdom flourished, and his immediate successor was the most highly exalted king Israel had ever seen (1 Chronicles 29:25). Since David honored God and didn't allow the mistakes of his predecessor to be found in his successor, Solomon didn't have to deal with the mistakes of Saul. Solomon was enabled to walk directly into the purpose that God had in store for him, and God was able to fulfill the works he began in David through Solomon (1 Kings 6:12).

I may not know you personally, and it's true that I don't completely know your background. It may sound unfair to be the one who is left to build the foundation of a path that your parents should have built. Honestly, you're right. Your parents should have built it, but guess what—they didn't. You can't change what your predecessors did or didn't do. All you can determine is what *you* do. You may think, *Aaron, you don't know my life. You don't know what I faced growing up. You don't know my hurts.* Yes, true. Even if we are best friends, there is no way I could actually feel the hurt you feel that was inflicted on you by your predecessors. It may feel like an unwanted burden to build a foundation from nothing, but it is incredibly necessary. You may have been physically, emotionally, or even sexually abused as a child. And perhaps you feel it's all you can do to simply get yourself to live with that every day. Why should you be the one to have to carry a cross and build a foundation when no one else would? It's because no matter what hurt you felt and no matter what you were handed, your children don't deserve to inherit the same hurt you bear. If you were the one willing to lay down all of the hurt to focus on the one thing that matters, which is constructing a life that leads directly to the Father's heart, you would change your life and those of the generations to follow. The future generations deserve a well-constructed path that will lead them to the Father's heart. No, it may not seem fair. Then again, it wasn't exactly fair that Jesus took up a cross because of Adam's decision. That one act of taking up a cross to lay a foundation to the Father's heart for us changed the world forever.

CONFIDENCE ON THE PATH

INSTANT GRATIFICATION

As you read, you may be thinking, *This guy is making this purpose thing sound pretty simple. Why would I ever get discouraged on this path? If God makes me a promise, He will never break that promise, so I know I have nothing to worry about. I'll go from promise to purpose! Easy.*

Theoretically, yes. When I was in college, I majored in electrical engineering, and that was a word you heard a ton—theoretical. The true definition of theoretical is "concerned with or involving the theory of a subject or area of study rather than its practical application."[12] Basically, it's what you expect the outcome to be in a perfect world. In this perfect world, when God made you a promise, you would immediately step into that purpose. Next thing you know, you're changing the world. I need you to know this: when God makes you a promise, He will deliver, and you will change the world, but it isn't instant.

Let me ask you this: What tastes better, a pizza that you heat up in the microwave for a couple minutes or a pizza coming out of the oven at Slice? (Slice is a local Birmingham pizza place. Probably the best in town and a 10/10 on the "If you ask Aaron" app.) (*Disclaimer: "If you ask Aaron" is not a real app.*) That pizza coming out of the microwave is definitely quicker than getting in your car, driving downtown, finding a parking space, waiting to be seated, ordering, and then waiting some more on this pizza, but is the microwave pizza really better? It's ready in two minutes, sure, but the crust tastes more like cardboard than bread. The cheese isn't really on the pizza. It somehow magically vanishes as it's cooked in the microwave. I mean, it seems to make sense: if you're hungry, the sooner you eat, the better. That's not always the case. The patience to eat something worthwhile when you're hungry leaves you more fulfilled than instant gratification. God's purpose in your life is the same way. When God makes a promise, He will most certainly deliver, but that doesn't mean it's going to happen right here and now. The reason is that you wouldn't be ready for your purpose.

There's a saying by Rick Yancey: "God doesn't always call the equipped, but He always equips the called" (author's paraphrase). If you're called to fulfill a purpose, God will equip you, but you have to allow Him the time to do so.

If you've ever been in this season of life where you're allowing God to equip you, you know how straight frustrating this time can be. You know and believe in what God has promised you, but you're stuck in what feels like a faith limbo waiting on what the Lord needs to instill in you before you can move into your purpose.

WHO DO YOU TRUST?

I want you, for a moment, to place your minds back on the children of Israel walking through the desert. They knew that they were called to inherit a promised land. God had even made momentous events take place to remove their bondage. The children of Israel were literally walking on the path to their purpose. So why were they wandering around the desert just hoping to walk into the promise of God?

If we begin to read in Numbers 14, we see Caleb, Joshua, and ten other spies that went to scout the land they were promised. When they returned with the report of giants dwelling in the land, the Israelites couldn't understand why the God that brought them out of slavery would place an obstacle in their way so giant (pun intended) that they couldn't walk straight into their promised inheritance. You see though, it wasn't God changing His mind or even changing His plan or purpose. It was an opportunity to show faith in the promise God had made. Faith that no matter what the path looked like, the Lord would provide and deliver His promise.

Rather than having faith in the site of hardship, the other ten spies spread discouraging rumors among the people that the giants residing in the land were too powerful and the walls too strong. Caleb attempted to walk in courage and told the people, "We should go up and take possession of the land, for we can certainly do it." As Caleb walked in courage, the other ten said, "We can't attack those people; they are stronger than we are" (Numbers 13:30–31). Israel stood as one body to decide whether to trust God or trust their instincts. The body was split between those that believe and have courage and those that had serious doubt the promise was ever real.

This directly translates to our lives. When we stand in front of the last but largest obstacle before we inherit the promise of God, we must make a decision. It's the same decision Israel faced. Will you believe in God or yourself? Israel had the chance to trust and inherit the promised land, but instead, they became timid in their faith. They couldn't believe the promise made to them could be kept in such dire conditions. It is vital to have faith; when God commits a promise to you, He will, beyond any circumstance or doubt, pull through and make good on His promise. Notice, I didn't say you should always *feel* God will make good on His promise. I said have faith. Faith is not a feeling but is what you *know* to be true. Even when you can't see, you know.

Because of their disbelief in God's promise, the Israelites didn't attack the land, which means they did not get to walk into the promised land. Instead, they wandered around the desert for forty years. Israel's wandering came by their own choice. If the Israelites' faith and courage in God would have been present that day, the promise could have been theirs. The unhealthy spirit in the body of Israel stopped them from taking the land; the children of Israel had to go back into preparation—into the desert. There still was some equipping that needed to occur before they could walk into the promise as one body. The children of Israel did not wander around because of God's anger and punishment. They wandered out of His care and love for them. If the children of Israel would have invaded the land on the day of their disbelief, they would have been slain. If the nation of Israel is slain that day, the story of the Bible and the lineage of Jesus stops there. Out of the love and sovereignty of God, He isolated Israel to remove the unhealthy part of the Body that would cause their demise. God didn't shut the door that day on His promise but rather worked the disbelief for the good of the children of Israel (Romans 8:28).

There will be times when our faith is tested. We come to a crossroad of totally believing God and His sovereignty or choosing to focus on what stands in the way of that promise. Sometimes we don't choose the correct action; we're human, and our disbelief can overwhelm us—just like a certain disciple who accomplished what no other ordinary man has by walking on water (i.e., Peter). Even as he was literally walking in a miracle, he became distracted with all the reasons why the act of walking on water shouldn't be happening and began to drown. However, even when Peter focused on the wrong thing, Jesus was focused on Peter. Jesus wasn't harsh with Peter, and he wasn't enraged at Peter's lack of dependency. He simply reached down and picked Peter up. Jesus loves us, and He is patient with us. Could we have walked into the promise of our purpose that God spoke into our lives had we believed? Yes. But we didn't, and that kills us as we feel that door closing in our face. However, when doors close in our lives, it doesn't make the identity that God has called us to be any weaker, but it makes your purpose that He has called you to stronger.

We see the difficult and discomforting path Israel took because of their decision, but what could have happened if they had believed? Yes, there is grace when we fall short in faith, but what kind of purpose would we walk into if we believe? Years after giants stood between Israel and the promise God had spoken, there was another giant standing in the way of God's promised purpose to Israel. Goliath called out,

> *Choose a man and have him come down to me. If he is able to fight and kill me, we will become your subjects; but if I overcome him and kill him, you will become our subjects and serve us.* (1 Samuel 17:30)

Israel wasn't just facing a hard time; they were on the brink of slavery once again. It was a different captor, but the past had come back to face them. I could imagine being in their situation, thinking, *I suppose the promise of God was only for a season*, feeling that the freedom was only for a moment, soon to be bound again. Just one problem, though: Jesus doesn't give temporary freedom! It is eternal, always eternal, freedom.

Hearing Goliath's challenge to Israel, they were terrified. Goliath repeated this for forty days, and every morning, the army of Israel ran in fear. Young David wasn't in the army. He was only bringing some bread and cheese to the commander and his army. When David heard Goliath's speech, he was appalled that someone would defy God like that. When David began to ask the other soldiers about Goliath, his oldest brother became enraged and said to him,

> *Why have you come down here? And with whom did you leave those few sheep in the wilderness? I know how conceited you are and how wicked your heart is.* (1 Samuel 17:28)

All right, first, who says that to anyone? In every way, he insulted David. It wasn't enough to call him conceited and wicked, but he even insulted David as a shepherd by saying how small his herd was. His oldest brother basically just told David that he was worthless. David ignored him and told King Saul, "Let no one lose heart on account of this Philistine; your servant will go and fight him." That's some boldness. Saul replied, "You are not able to go out against this Philistine and fight him" (1 Samuel 17: 32–33). So, in a few verses, David has been called worthless and told he isn't good enough. This would be enough reason for anyone to bail. However, David saw this moment and recognized the purpose. He responded to Saul,

> *Your servant has been keeping his father's sheep. When a lion or a bear came and carried off a sheep from the flock, I went after it, struck it and rescued the sheep from its mouth. When it turned on me, I seized it by its hair, struck it and killed it ... The Lord who rescued me from the paw of the lion and the paw of the bear will rescue me from the hand of this Philistine. (1 Samuel 17:34–35, 37)*

David didn't back down from the God moment. David recognized the promise and walked forward in faith. Had he listened to his own instincts that day, David would have believed his brother and Saul. David would have believed he was worthless and not good enough. I believe this is a relatable story. We spend too much time listening to the wrong voice, which declares we are unworthy and unwanted. Then we base our life decisions on that voice. Listening to the wrong voice can cause us to miss out on some major promises. This isn't uncommon, though. It's only natural to focus on the loudest thing that we hear; however, the loudest noise is not always God's voice.

David chose to disregard the loud, negative voices. His faith was not timid; it was bold. He walked out in such faith that he took off the armor Saul had given him. Once he was on the battlefield facing Goliath, the giant began to belittle him. David heard a loud voice telling him once again he wasn't good enough. His response:

> *"This day the Lord will deliver you into my hands, and I'll strike you down and cut off your head ... The battle is the Lord's." (1 Samuel 17:46, 47)*

David claimed the victory before his enemy! He declared the victory over his obstacle (a large, violent obstacle). As Goliath came closer, David ran toward Goliath. David didn't stall to strategize a certain battle plan, and he didn't hesitate to stop and ponder that he might die in three seconds. David threw only one stone. Not only did the Lord deliver Israel from the threat of an enemy after Goliath fell, but the army of Israel slayed the Philistine army in complete victory. Everything the Philistines had in their camps now belonged to the Israelites.

When your obstacle or enemy sees the strength of God, it will run in terror. Nothing will ever stand to the strength of God Almighty. The same decision was there for Israel when they were going to inherit the land as there was for David. Do I have confidence in God's promised purpose for me, or do I have confidence in myself?

REMEMBER YOUR ANOINTING

It can be difficult, as we walk on our path, not to become envious of another's purpose. We see David walking out on a battlefield, decapitating giants, and we're the ones standing in the back just getting to haul the armor of the king. To put it in today's language, we see a quarterback drive the length of the field to win a championship, and maybe we're just the equipment manager. Both get a championship ring symbolizing that both contributed to the victory; however, inside, we know how much we contributed to win the ring. We may not feel as important as the quarterback hoisted on the backs of teammates with the trophy raised in the air. We may even feel slightly embarrassed to even own the ring because the efforts we contributed were not parallel to the superstar MVP. If you think about it, though, without the equipment manager, would any of the necessary equipment to play the game even get to the stadium? Probably not, because the equipment manager had a purpose to fulfill on the team, even if it wasn't glamorous. If the equipment manager didn't get the equipment to the desired destination, then he wouldn't have completed his called-upon purpose.

We all have a called purpose in this life; a specific anointing. Some view your calling as insignificant, yet others consider your calling desirable. All of our purposes make up one body of Christ, which will continue the ministry He began on earth. If we are too busy believing that our purpose is insignificant, the body will become sick and malfunction; it will begin to break down. For the ministry of Christ to prevail and go forth into the world, each of us must have complete confidence in what we are called to do. This confidence comes through the security of who God has created you to be. Where there is lack of security in your calling, a door opens to doubt the anointing God has divinely placed upon your life. Doubting the anointing of your life allows your heart to be vulnerable.

Vulnerability isn't bad. It's important to be open and vulnerable to the One who desires complete access to your heart for the betterment of your eternal soul. That kind of vulnerability makes your heart available to the purpose of God and the advancement of His ministry. Vulnerability caused by doubt is different. This vulnerability allows the opinions of others to dictate the anointing you operate in. In short, you lose confidence in who you are created to be. Your heart, in turn, begins to depend on the opinions and validation of others. This is incredibly dangerous; your self-worth will slowly hinge on these validating opinions. Don't get me wrong; it's a great feeling to have. It's almost like a high to see how many compliments and endorsements pour in from others. But there are two routes to take:

Route 1: Those around you take the time and attention to validate you because they love you and care about your self-worth. This is awesome, right? Well, kind of. It's awesome because they have the patience to put up with all the times you need a confidence boost. Just a little insight: dude, it's annoying. While some never see this side of the situation, it can cause damage to the majority of the relationships you're in because there will be times in others' lives that the other half of the relationship needs help and support. You can become so obsessed trying to get compliments out of them that you neglect their needs. Bitterness and resentment will take root in their hearts against you. However, say you leech your friends dry without causing resentment in their hearts (if you do, that special individual is a way better friend than me) and you are full of other's compliments. Where is the room in your heart for the validation of Christ's blood, the only validation that truly matters?

Route 2: Those around you seem like quite terrible people, and the validations don't come. This does happen in life, for whatever reason. Some relationships are difficult, and compliments don't exactly flow like milk and honey in the promised land. Those folks around you aren't terrible. Perhaps they didn't receive the validation they needed and they don't know how to give what they've never received. When validations don't come, it may feel as if there is a void. If this feeling continues, depression is a real possibility. Your heart is never uplifted, so you feel low, sometimes like trash. Or you may not become depressed, but you become disappointed in others. That disappointment (planted out of your own insecurities) produces bitterness that, if not dealt with, will become a calloused wall around your heart.

Both routes lead to the same place: Where is there room in the heart for Christ's blood? The void has already been filled by either the validations of others or bitterness toward others. Both lack security, which, in turn, hinders hearts from growing in the Father and walking deeper into their purpose.

I began my college career at a small community college where I completed my core classes (took that ACT five times but could never get a score that started with a 2). I transferred to UAB (Blaze On!) my third year and started taking classes that were specific to my degree. As I've said before, my major was electrical engineering, so it was a big jump for me to go from taking English and Literature to Circuits 101 and Digital Logic. To say I struggled my first semester would be an incredible understatement. The material wasn't coming easy to me, and I was frustrated. I did well in all my classes outside of engineering. I made high grades in the calculus classes I had taken, but that didn't transfer over to my engineering classes. I can still remember staring at the white board not having a single clue what that Jamaican professor was even talking about. I just knew to nod my head when he turned around to ensure no one would know my secret—that I was as lost as a Hebrew in the desert. I was a proactive student, though (even if I wasn't bold enough to let the entire class know I was struggling), so I went to meet with the professor privately one day after class. As I walked into his cluttered office stacked with boxes and research papers, I began to explain my struggle with understanding the material. Throughout our conversation, he essentially told me there were signs I might not make a good engineer. Being a perfectionist (obviously my emotional health was 10/10), I took immediate offense to that. From that moment until the time I graduated, three years later, I used the voice of that one professor, hinting that I might not be a great engineer to motivate me throughout my degree. I stopped taking classes to just understand application and to better myself; instead, I studied and worked with the intent to prove that one professor wrong. Now, if you went back to that professor and asked him about all this, he would more than likely have no recollection of that instance. I allowed one sentence to control my mindset for four years. You may be thinking, *Didn't he say it took him three years to finish school?* Yes, yes it did. I say that one sentence controlled my life for four years because I took it into the workforce with me after college. I was still attempting to prove that I was smart enough. I already had the degree, so that should have been enough, right? It wasn't. I wanted even strangers to tell me how smart I was. Understand, this didn't come out of a place of conceit. This came from doubting my anointing.

I didn't take the type of job out of college that came easy to me. I went and found the most difficult, mind-boggling job I could find and tried to prove I was good enough. Spoiler: it did not work. My life was miserable! I was attempting to operate outside of my anointing by putting my confidence in the validation from my boss. In short, the employment fell swimmingly short, and my life and confidence were crushed. When you operate outside of your anointing by seeking the approval and validation of others, your heart becomes vulnerable to being crushed at any moment. Like the Sunday school song used to sing, "The foolish man built his house upon the sand, and the rain came tumbling down."[25] The rain is going to come down in your life, and that is the one truth you can't argue with. When it does come down, how's your foundation? Is it rock solid, or is it unstable? If you're seeking the validation of others to fuel your anointing, you will fall.

> *Do not pay attention to every word people say, or you may hear your servant crushing you—for you know in your heart that many times you yourself have cursed others. (Ecclesiastes 7:21–22)*

If you, out of your own mouth, crush others, how can you depend on another imperfect human to give validity to your purpose? It's like the blind leading the blind! They honestly have no idea. Instead, would it not be wiser to build your foundation on a God that loves you and has anointed you to complete an exact purpose (Jeremiah 29:11, Romans 8:28)? Here's the thing: it takes less of you to walk in your anointing than to walk in the validation of others. Think about it. When your life consists of obtaining high praise, there is a never-ending, exhausting effort that is necessary to meet the expectations of others. If you choose to humbly walk in your God-anointed purpose, then there is only one person in your life to please. His name is Jesus, and He already died for you before you even realized you needed saving. Something gives me the hint that you might be able to please Him. All that is necessary to please him is you—*all of you*. Look at the poor widow in Mark 12:41–43.

> *Jesus sat down opposite the place where the offerings were put and watched the crowd putting their money into the temple treasury. Many rich people threw in large amounts. But a poor widow came and put in two very small copper coins, worth only a few cents. Calling his disciples to him, Jesus said, "Truly I tell you, this poor widow has put more into the treasury than all the others.*

They gave out of their wealth; but she, out of her poverty, put in everything—all she had to live on."

It's not a requirement that your purpose be equivalent to anyone else's or that others agree with your anointing. This poor widow, who had next to nothing, gave all she had so there was nothing left to her name. I'm sure others were disapproving of her financially poor decision, but she caught the eye of Jesus. Jesus wasn't impressed with all the rich giving out of overflow; rather, He instructed His disciples to live like this woman who gave the most—all that she had.

Jesus gave all of Himself to fulfill His purpose. Even when He had nothing left to give, He gave himself, selflessly, in confidence. See, Jesus wasn't crucified with the guarantee of you loving Him. The Son of God didn't wait until He received your love to walk into the most daunting purpose of all. Jesus did all He did in confidence. Jesus allowed soldiers to pierce His head with thorns and demolish his flesh at a whipping post. He carried a cross that weighed heavy on His back because of the sin you and I committed. He surrendered His hands to be hung on a cross, to die a guilty man's death in humiliation. The King took His last breath beaten and unrecognizable. *In confidence.* Jesus didn't just die; Jesus died in confidence of the Father's will and goodness. He died in confidence that when He laid down His life, His Father would resurrect Him which would make a way for the resurrection of you and me.

STAMINA ON THE PATH

THE MIDDLE

To all my marathon runners out there, I applaud you. I haven't personally participated in a marathon (unless you count a 5 k) because I believe there has to be something disconnected in the head to run an incredible distance willingly without your life hanging in the balance (especially when another option is donuts; always remember, if available, eat the donut). If you are one of "those people" who run marathons, this word will probably be quite relatable to you: stamina. Just hearing the word might take you to a moment in one of your races when you needed that stamina to have the ability to sustain your pace. Focus on that moment. For the donut eaters like me who haven't ran a marathon, think about a moment where you felt overwhelmed by the race you were running in life. Maybe it's your career, maybe it's school, or maybe it's your walk with Jesus. In whatever race you're part of, what is the most difficult part of accomplishing your goal? What is the most difficult part of getting to the finish line? It's that portion of the race where you realize you are in the exact middle. It's that moment when the pain starts to sink in, the side starts to cramp, and your mind starts to explain to you that running this far was a terrible idea. You're exhausted and start to think that you can't continue.

There are going to be times like this along the path of your purpose. You started out like a champ! Running and fist-pumping, exclaiming the glory of God and shouting His promise of your purpose to anyone who would listen. You get to the second leg of the path, and you slow down a bit, but you're still encouraged. You still believe! Then you realize just how long you've been running. Shouldn't you be finished with this race by now? Or shouldn't you at least feel more encouraged than you did when you began this race? Usually you don't. It's usually during this time that you feel the most beat down, that you feel the most discouraged, that you feel hopelessness beginning to sink into your bones. Your body suddenly becomes so much heavier. It's difficult to even keep your feet stepping, much less running!

So, there was this dude in the Bible. It's possible you've heard of him. His name is Joseph. If you're not familiar, he's the Technicolor coat guy. Joseph was the youngest son of eleven. He was incredibly favored by his father—more than any of his brothers (Genesis 37:3). While Joseph might have been his father's favorite, it is safe to say he was the least favorite among his brothers. His brothers absolutely detested him and refused to speak a word to him (Genesis 37:4).

Joseph communicated with God in a unique way. He was a dreamer. Like most every movie, the dreamer wasn't taken seriously (side note: it's my personal opinion that people are afraid to take dreamers seriously because that would mean letting go of the comfort of their own realities long enough to believe something else could be better). Joseph had a dream that essentially showed his brothers bowing down to him. Joseph thought it would be a good idea to tell his brothers this amazing news (Genesis 37:9).

> Then he had another dream, and he told it to his brothers. "Listen," he said, "I had another dream, and this time the sun and moon and eleven stars were bowing down to me."

His brothers were not cool with bowing down to the runt of the litter (shocker), so the brothers, in the most loving way possible, came up with a plot to even the playing field: they plotted to kill him (Genesis 37:18–19). Let's keep it real here. How would you respond if your punk little brother came up to you and said, "One day, you will bow to me"? I'm a little brother, and I can assure you that a plan to kill me would have been nice in comparison to what my brother would have done. The oldest of the brothers, Reuben, had a kind enough heart to step forward and suggest that they "only" throw him in the cistern, which is like a well. To Reuben's credit, he was trying to save Joseph's life and not end up in the cistern with him. Later in the night when Reuben wasn't around, Joseph's brothers were sharing a meal and had a change of heart (Genesis 37:26).

> *Judah said to his brothers, "What will we gain if we kill our brother and cover up his blood?"*

I can imagine Joseph sitting in the bottom of this dark, damp cistern, hearing his brothers come to their senses and realize that they shouldn't kill him and beginning to feel everything was going to be all right. But that only lasts about four seconds, until Judah begins to speak again (Genesis 37:27).

> *Come, let's sell him to the Ishmaelites and not lay your hands on him; after all, he is our brother, our own flesh and blood.*

When Reuben comes back, he flips his lid because he was actually trying to save Joseph and get him back to his father. Finding themselves in a bit of a bind, the brothers faked Joseph's death so their father would think Joseph was dead (Genesis 37:31). Joseph didn't exactly have things going his way. So, to recap, Joseph received a dream, or a promise if you will, that his brothers would bow down to him. Joseph was encouraged and excited. Now he is sold into slavery and his brothers have faked his death so his father wouldn't come looking for him. This probably wasn't Joseph's best day ever.

In spite of the terrible way his life was heading, Joseph found favor. He was living in the Pharaoh's household, and things were looking up. It was a terrible way of getting to this place, but now Joseph has made it to his promise, right? He's living in the palace, high up in the house of Pharaoh. So the dream he had of his brothers bowing down was a figurative promise. The dream proved God would put him in a position of power, right? Well, actually, no. God is a God who means what He says and says what He means. If He gives you a promise, He will deliver that exact promise. Joseph isn't at the finish line of his purpose yet.

Pharaoh's wife was the only thing in the kingdom not allowed to Joseph. Joseph was "well-built and handsome" (Genesis 39:6). After a while, ole wifey notices that tight bod; she begins to think that she would rather have Joseph than her husband, so she attempts to seduce Joseph day after day (Genesis 39:10). Like the man of God Joseph was, he resisted every time. One day, when no one was around, Pharaoh's wife grabbed Joseph's cloak in an attempt to seduce him. As Joseph escaped her cougar claws, she ripped his cloak off. The wife of Pharaoh had framed Joseph. Pharaoh, obviously outraged, throws Joseph in prison. Things are looking bleak once more in Joseph's life. It would have been quite easy for Joseph to give up at this point and believe he had simply misheard the message from heaven. However, *God moved.* Joseph found favor in the eyes of the prison warden, and he could do as he pleased (Genesis 39:23).

One morning, Joseph awoke to two of his prison mates losing their minds. They both had dreams with no clue of their meaning. Since Joseph had not given up on God's purpose, he was still hearing from heaven, and he was able to interpret the dreams of the men (Genesis 40:12,13). The interpretations came to be true, and one of the men returned to his original position—the house of Pharaoh. Joseph requested that his cellmate remember him and to get him out of the prison. The man, once freed and back to his original position, forgot about Joseph. It was two years before his cellmate remembered what

Joseph had done for him, two years that Joseph waited solely on hope. That takes sincere perseverance in a promise. One day, the Pharaoh had a dream that disturbed him, and the freed prisoner working in Pharaoh's household remembered someone who could interpret dreams—Joseph. Joseph was brought to Pharaoh and interpreted the dream. The Pharaoh was so pleased with this interpretation, he made Joseph second in command of Egypt (Genesis 41:40). Joseph had so much power that no one could breathe without his say so. The interpretation Joseph gave for the Pharaoh's dream was that there would be seven years of great prosperity and seven years of severe famine. At Joseph's command, the kingdom withheld a fifth of the harvest during the seven years of prosperity so that they would have enough to outlast the famine. The famine, however, extended throughout the land; families traveled from all over to ask for food, even Joseph's brothers. Remember the brothers who sold Joseph into slavery and disguised his disappearance with death? Yes. Those brothers. So Joseph is staring into the faces of blood relatives who attempted to ruin his life all because they were jealous of his favor. They have no idea that the man they are speaking to is Joseph. As it dawns on Joseph's brothers that they are speaking to the governor of the land (i.e., Joseph) every brother bows in a sign of respect, just as in Joseph's dream, just as in God's promise.

I'm sure when Joseph first received this promise, he envisioned himself being in some sort of power, but he never could have never imagined the difficulty it took to get there. When we receive a promise from God, we have an image of what that promise will look like but get discouraged when the promise doesn't happen in the way we see it. Where would have Joseph's life been if the promise of God had played out as he envisioned it? Who knows? But he probably would not have risen as high as the governor of Egypt. How would Joseph's life have turned out if he got frustrated every time the purpose of God didn't meet his mental expectations? That man would have lived in a constant state of frustration and more than likely settled for a seasonal moment instead of the great purpose God planned for him. This is why it is important to have spiritual stamina. Stamina will give us the endurance to understand that God has put a promise in us even when we're tired of waiting on Him to bring it out of us.

SETTLING FOR SOUP

There's a book by Mark Rutland called *David the Great*.[13] If you haven't read it, you should. The book moves you through David's life in detail: the highs and lows, the good and the terrible. As I read this book, one part of David's life stuck out to me. I had heard about this and read over it in the Bible, but I never really understood why this part of David's life was recorded. David was essentially a mercenary for the Philistines, which was pretty much the archrival of Israel. During this time, he became king of a city called Ziklag. David was anointed at a very young age to be king, and after enduring pure misery, David was finally king. I'm sure it went through David's mind: "Well, I was anointed king. Guess this is it. Not at all what I thought God promised, but here I am. I mean, it does make sense. I'm just a kid shepherd who was anointed king. I should have known it wouldn't be of Israel."

I'll be transparent with you: I've had similar feelings. I've felt God plant a seed of promise in me and then felt completely disappointed when I walked into what I thought was the fulfillment of that promise. This feeling of disappointment can make it extremely tempting not to walk out the promise to its fulfillment. We build up a moment in our heads only to feel slightly let down. We thought that surely this was going to be the moment where we walked into our purpose, but it isn't so.

The short of it is we grow tired of waiting on what's to come by focusing only on what is right in front of us. We're enticed to give up. No one actually admits this, and you'd never see an inspirational poster of that cute little cat letting go of the ledge and a caption that reads, "Just give up."

Isn't it true, though? How many times do we feel like giving up? Better yet, how many times do we give up? "Often" would be my answer, but we don't use the trigger words "quit" or "give up." We mask our failure by calling it "settling." How often do we make New Year's resolutions, saying, "Man, I'd kill to be in shape. No excuses! This is the year." It's about day three when we realize there's a reason that so few people sport *Avengers*-sculpted bodies. It takes work. Honestly, though, it isn't the work that scares people away. It's more so the duration of the work—the stamina.

Stamina takes work, and that is the exact reason few people have it—or, should I say, keep it. Living a life on stamina is difficult because it means we must lay down our temporal pleasures for eternal gain when human nature screams at our brain cells to settle. Receiving a promise and walking into a purpose would be easy if it all happened in a day, but even kings don't inherit the throne when they're born, even if it is their birthright.

Back in the days of old, Isaac and his wife gave birth to twins: Jacob and Esau. You could say Jacob and Esau were a bit different. Esau was a man's man, who "became a skillful hunter." On the other hand Jacob "was content to stay at home among the tents" (Genesis 25:27). Essentially, Isaac was a momma's boy, while Esau walked in his father's shadow. It's important to know here that Esau was the first born. The reason? Oh, nothing much, just that the first born was promised to be the one in charge and would receive the blessing of the father. "Under the ordinary circumstances, the younger of the two sons would be subservient to the older"(Genesis 25:23, footnote).[3] So, in short, even though the boys were twins, Esau was to receive the blessing of the father because he popped out seven seconds before Isaac. Either way, it was Esau's birthright to inherit his father's blessing. We see later (in Genesis 27:28–29) just what Isaac had purposed for his son.

> *May God give you heaven's dew and earth's richness—an abundance of grain and new wine. May nations serve you and peoples bow down to you. Be lord over your brothers, and may the sons of your mother bow down to you. May those who curse you be cursed and those who bless you be blessed.*

Every bit of that spoken blessing was Esau's. It was his birthright to accept or reject. God places callings on us to walk into; but unless we accept them, the calling remains ineffective.

Esau rolled in from the "open country" one day famished from all his manly man deeds (Genesis 25: 29). He got a waft of the stew Jacob was cooking and demanded, "Quick, let me have some of that red stew! I'm famished!" (Genesis 25:30). Esau had a serious problem on his hands. He was hangry. I mean, I get that. I'm ashamed to say what I do when I'm hungry enough.

But Jacob had a proposal: "First sell me your birthright" (Genesis 25:31). Esau, in terribly dramatic fashion, replied, "Look, I'm about to die, what good is the birthright to me?" (Genesis 25:32). Esau agreed to Jacob's proposal. The man literally sold his birthright for a bowl of soup. Some pride and joy he was to his father. This seems ridiculous and a bit extreme, I know. However, think about this: How many times have you considered or actually gone through with an action you knew would hinder your calling? Maybe it was a significant other in college you couldn't say no to. Perhaps it was a party you just had to attend. It doesn't even have to be that obvious. Maybe it's that sneaky TV watching you did last night when no one else would find out. Whatever your bowl of soup has been in your life, has it ever really been worth it? In the moments you've been hangry for the pleasures of this world, where you have demanded to be fed, has it ever been worth it in the end? Was it ever worth settling? The enticing thought of settling is appealing. Settling is accepting empty actions in replacement of a God-given birthright. Settling trades eternal gain for temporal pleasures.

In Matthew 7:13–14, Jesus points out,

> *Enter through the narrow gate. For wide is the gate and broad is the road that leads to destruction, and many enter through it. But small is the gate and narrow the road that leads to life, and only a few find it*

Look, this path we walk on is narrow, and it can be exhausting. To truly walk on this path, we have to allow ourselves to die daily, not to settle. We must have the stamina not to grow tired of living our life for God's glory and not to settle for our passing pleasures.

It's difficult to stay focused when walking on a narrow path, especially when the path seems endlessly difficult. Remember that moment in David's life we were talking about? David was anointed to be king of Israel, but he was stuck as king of a Philistine city. Honestly, by this point in David's life, I would've given up and given up hard. I would've stayed in the cave when Saul was chasing me, started calling myself the "Cave King," and claimed that as the promise. It seems ridiculous, but it's honestly what most of us do. We know we aren't where God promised us we would be, but we're tired of trying to find the end of this path, so we just stop and call it promise. What if David stopped and called Ziklag the promise? He never would have had the correct throne to hand over to Solomon. He would have had a throne, sure, but that throne wouldn't have allowed the purpose of God to be fulfilled all the way to Jesus. Mark Rutland says this about David's moment in Ziklag:

> *Beware of the close substitute, and do not forget God's call on your life that was once so clear. Tell God, "I'm at Ziklag right now, Lord, because this is where you have placed me, but my hands are open. I will not clutch this moment to my breast and scream, 'Mine, mine, mine!' It's all Yours. Do with it and me what you will."* [13]

Neither David nor Joseph gave into their hangry pleasures and settled for anything less than the exact promise that God had given them. They had the stamina to wait on the true purpose.

OWN YOUR PURPOSE

Have you ever stopped to wonder why Joseph told his brothers and parents the dream he had? Unless he was the cockiest punk-teenager who ever lived, why would he tell the people who provided him food and shelter that they would bow to him? Was it just a power trip? Obviously, I don't know Joseph, but trying to make people submit to his "power" doesn't line up with his character. Also, if he had these egotistical issues, God probably wouldn't have called him to a place of power. I believe Joseph simply wasn't intimidated by the greatness of his purpose from God, the same as David. David was never intimidated by the "giant" purpose God called him to (pun intended). Notice in both Joseph and David's lives: when they began to either tell others about their purpose or walk in their purpose, those closest to them tried to tell them they were wrong. It is entirely possible that the family members discouraging these two men could have been solely out of love. You know, the whole "Don't get your hopes too high, kid" mentality. But here's the cool thing about God: we can get our hopes up because He has already made way for what He has promised. What God has ordained, no man can hinder in any way (Isaiah 43:13). Maybe it was in their innocence, but David and Joseph seemed to understand this, and it was the key to their stamina. They didn't allow the discouragement of those closest to them to move their mind off of what God had promised.

Side note: if you're a young adult reading this, understand, I am not saying to reject counsel. Counsel is needed, and is the thing that keeps us grounded. However, when you begin to walk into your purpose, it's entirely possible for those around you to discourage you out of envy. But just like Joseph and David, you shouldn't be timid about the favor God displays in your life. Own that favor! Be bold! It takes boldness to have stamina while waiting on a purpose that isn't quite yet a reality. It took boldness for Noah to build a boat on dry ground. But be aware: the discouragement of those around you makes the path that much harder to keep moving forward. This is when the rubber meets the road, as they say. In other words, this is where your endurance is tested. Do you have the stamina to keep believing in a promise when all you have is that promise? When everything else begins to fall around you and the path becomes more difficult to find, would you have the endurance to continue believing?

WHY ARE WE RUNNING?

It is incredibly difficult to convince yourself to continue when you're in the middle of a race. When you can't look back and see the starting point and too far away to see the finish line. Your side is doing some sort of weird cramping thing, and for some reason, your shoulder is cramping too. Is that just me? Your legs feel as strong as cooked noodles, and you'd kill for a rest. This is the breaking point. Your mind really begins to wander this time. "Do I have enough in me? Did I train hard enough for this? Is my leg going to fall off?" It's this moment that defines how we finish the race. In our weakest hour, how would we respond? Let me remind you of two things:

1. We are not running this race to satisfy ourselves.
2. If we allow our weakest moments to be covered in God's grace, there will be endurance unending.

If we were running this race to satisfy ourselves, I would have picked a much easier race to run, or I might not have run at all. We don't take part in this marathon purpose to satisfy our needs but to allow God's kingdom to have its way in our lives. Paul paints this for us in Philippians 3:12–14.

> *Not that I have already obtained all this, or have already arrived at my goal, but I press on to take hold of that for which Christ Jesus took hold of me. Brothers and sisters, I do not consider myself yet to have taken hold of it. But one thing I do: Forgetting what is behind and straining toward what is ahead, I press on toward the goal to win the prize for which God has called me heavenward in Christ Jesus.*

Paul realized the honest truth about this race we run: it feels miserable sometimes. It can feel heavy and discouraging, yet Paul was encouraged. Why? Paul realized the endurance he had inside him was not actually *of* him because the race was not *for* him. He kept running toward his "goal" (his purpose) because he remembered why he was running. He was running for the reason Christ Jesus created him.

OUR FOCUS

Even when we realize why we are running the race, how do we remind ourselves not to settle? How do we choose to not grow complacent in our one focus? Paul says in 1 Corinthians 9:24,

> *Run in such a way as to get the prize. … I do not fight like a boxer beating the air. No, I strike a blow against my body and make it my slave so that after I have preached to others, I myself will not be disqualified for the prize.*

That's intense, bro. Paul reminds me of that personal trainer you are randomly assigned when you walk into the gym for the first time. You can about guarantee he's already thrown back like four shots of some barely legal steroid-laced pre-workout. He starts shouting stuff at you immediately, even during stretching. "We don't rest today! We push like we ain't never pushed!" Well, Paul seems to be shouting at us in 1 Corinthians, "You feel like settling? Strike a blow to your body!" I've actually taken this approach to Christianity, and I would love to let you in on the results I found. This approach doesn't work. Aaron, you're saying Paul, who wrote a good chunk of the New Testament, doesn't know what he's talking about? No, absolutely not. Paul was brilliant and had a zeal for Christ like few ever to live. Most people, including a younger me, might read this verse and think, "I have to stay completely intense at all times of my Christian walk to please the Lord so I can get my prize." It's the furthest thing from the truth. Paul simply tells us: don't settle.

When struggles tried to overpower Paul, he had the stamina to control his self-discipline to remind himself of why he was still walking this path—His eternal gain. Paul realized that to obtain the end "prize," there had to be a focus.

The countless distractions on the path require an intense amount of focus—an amount of focus God alone deserves. So, do we walk around speaking only of church services and Bible verses? No, we would never advance the ministry of Christ. With that mindset, the focus actually comes off the advancement of the kingdom of God and moves inward to the individual producing a "holy" enough path to be worthy of the prize. My dad always told me, "Never be so earthly minded that you're no heavenly good, but also never be so heavenly minded that you're no earthly good." If we weren't supposed to live on this earth and be a part of it, we wouldn't be here. I'm not saying go partake as the world partakes and blend in without boldness, but how are you to reach the "unholy" people if you are inwardly focused on obtaining a prize? I'll let Paul share his thoughts:

> *To the Jews I became like a Jew, to win the Jews. To those under the law I became like one under the law ... so as to win those under the law. To those not having the law I became like one not having the law ... so as to win those not having the law. ... I have become all things to all people so that by all possible means I might save someone. I do all this for the sake of the gospel, that I may share in it's blessing. (1 Corinthians 9:20–23)*

Do you know what I find interesting about this passage of Scripture? It's titled, "Paul's Use of His Freedom." Paul knew he had a purpose and a calling that would advance the ministry of Jesus and the kingdom of heaven. But Paul didn't walk around to those without the law quoting old scrolls showing how studious he was. Rather, he became like those people.

To understand the context of this, "those not having the law" were the Gentiles (1 Corinthians 9:21, footnote).[3] "Paul accommodated himself to the Gentile culture when it did not violate his allegiance to Christ" (1 Corinthians 9:21, footnote).[3] Paul wasn't going to those without the law to forget his Christian troubles and return to them on Sunday. On the contrary, he approached the situation with a focus on making the heart of Jesus known to the hearts of God's children.

I find it interesting that the next passage of Scripture is titled, "The Need for Self-Discipline." In this passage, Paul talks about striking yourself a blow and making your body a slave. So, in back-to-back passages, Paul speaks about obtaining an outward focus to advance the ministry of Jesus. Then he immediately speaks about the focus and discipline needed to completely walk in the fullness of his God-given purpose.

SECRET STRENGTH

So how does Paul keep going? It's easy to read this and think, *Oh, that's just Paul. He's one of them super Christians. I can't never get to his level.* False. God is not a respecter of persons. If He did it for Moses, He'll do it for you. If He did it for Paul, He'll do it for you. If He did it for Jesus, He'll do it for you. Paul had intense focus and determination not to settle in contentment. It seems contradictory to be content and not to settle, but the two could not be further apart. Settling will leave you dissatisfied and hungry for even further dissatisfaction. Contentment will transform your mindset past your current situations to understand the importance of eternal gain. Settling depends on the outcome of a situation, meaning that your joy and solace depend on the fulfillment of your *self* and its desires. Contentment detaches your dependence on the fulfillment of your flesh and places it on the fulfillment of Christ. If one truly lives in contentment, there wouldn't be married actions in a non-married environment. Rather, there would be trust that the season, no matter the emotion, would produce the purpose God has placed in your life. Paul says,

> *I have learned to be content whatever the circumstances. I know what it is to be in need, and I know what it is to have plenty. I have learned the secret of being content in any and every situation, whether well fed or hungry, whether living or in plenty or in want. I can do all this through him who gives me strength. (Philippians 4:11–13)*

Notice that in verse 12, Paul says he has "learned the secret of being content." Despite his intense focus on walking the path set before him, Paul understands that there's a secret to being content, and that there's a "strength" that allows him to do "all this." That secret strength is grace.

There was a time in Paul's life when he felt the heaviness of this path and the dissatisfaction of this world bearing down on him. He pleaded with God that the situation would be taken away from him. The Lord answered Paul in a different way from what Paul might have expected:

> *In order to keep me from becoming conceited, I was given a thorn in my flesh, a messenger of Satan, to torment me. Three times I pleaded with the Lord to take it away from me. But he said to me, "My grace is sufficient for you, for my power is made perfect in weakness." (2 Corinthians 12:7–9)*

In the moment when Paul pleaded that God would remove his heaviness, God said, "Hey, man, I know it's heavy, because I know you're weak. I made you. I know you. Why don't you go ahead and be weak. I work best when you're weak." Rather than removing Paul from the season of his weakness, God changed his mindset and heart by allowing Paul to understand that his strength (and even his situation) were irrelevant to the path he walked on. Paul goes on to say,

> *Therefore I will boast all the more gladly about my weaknesses, in insults, in hardships, in persecutions, in difficulties. For when I am weak, then I am strong. (2 Corinthians 12:9)*

So, where does Paul find his contentment? In God's sufficient grace. When choosing contentment, the action of settling disappears. Stamina develops, which produces the focus to obtain God's purpose and the contentment to accept Christ's grace.

The NLT translation says it this way:

> *My grace is all you need. My power works best in weakness. (NLT)*[14]

So simply put, God's grace is all you could ever need. His grace is the stamina. If you continue in the middle in this grace, there's hope. If you press on, there's a promise. If you endure, there's a purpose.

ISOLATION ON THE PATH

This may seem like a cliche question, but have you ever felt alone on your walk with Christ? Mentally, you know that Christ is beside you, but it still feels incredibly lonely. I'll be the first one to confess that I have felt exactly like this several times. In my loneliness, it's been extremely challenging to continue walking down this path. I still remember how dark and cold my soul was when I felt this loneliness. In the darkest times, I could always hear a voice saying, "Why keep going? Who is even here to walk beside you? Look how alone you are." This voice was always excruciatingly loud. However, there is one simple thing you need to know when you feel this way: you are not alone. That voice is a lie attempting to move you off the path. We humans were made for companionship, and we don't operate as intended when we are alone. This feeling is one of Satan's most frequently and efficiently used tactics. It can be described in one word: isolation.

LAND OF NOTHING

I was playing drums at a mission conference one weekend, and I began to pray that God would place a city on my heart to pray for and possibly go to. As I was praying, I felt God put a word in my heart: Cabul. I started searching for Cabul on the internet to get some insight and found out that Cabul is a place that is actually mentioned in the Bible. Cabul is the modern Kabul. [26] The word Kabul sounds like the Hebrew for "good-for-nothing" (subscript C in 1 Kings 9:13). Essentially, it means the "land of nothing." Kabul was a gift of land from King Solomon to Hiram. Hiram gave some financial backing in the construction of Solomon's temple, so Solomon wanted to reward him and gave Hiram twenty towns (1 Kings 9:11).

> *King Solomon gave twenty towns in Galilee to Hiram king of Tyre, because Hiram supplied him with all the cedar and juniper and gold he wanted.*

Hiram hated Solomon's gift. Hiram thought so little of it that he asked Solomon,

> *"What kind of towns are these you have given me, my brother?" he asked. And he called them the Land of Kabul, a name they have to this day. (1 Kings 9:13)*

As I read over this passage of Scripture, it brought a whole different thought to my head. Hiram gave in great measure and was repaid with "nothing." Maybe all you do is give and support, and at the end of it all, you feel like all you own is a land of nothing.

I imagine Moses felt this way when he signed up to be the protector of God's people only for them to reject and betray him (Exodus 2:14). I tend to focus on the latter part of Moses's life, but there is much to learn from the obscure beginning. Moses went from being in the running to rule Egypt to being an excommunicated outcast. How low would you feel if this happened to you? Could you imagine the loneliness? The shame? The isolation? I'm just saying, I would probably start to seriously doubt that I had a purpose in God's eyes.

Oh, let's just drop this in here: Moses hid in the obscurity for forty years. I understand that he lived longer than we do these days, and he wasn't just sitting there idly for half his life, but those forty years took the same amount of time to pass as they do now. Could you imagine what probably replayed in his mind during those forty years? He probably had thoughts playing in a loop in his mind, a loop of endless shame and regret. He probably saw himself killing the Egyptian, the accusation of his fellow Israelite, and the disappointment of the man who raised him. He likely had serious thoughts that he was not good enough, that he was a mistake to both the Egyptian and the Hebrew people, that he didn't belong anywhere—a feeling of isolation.

When I was a kid, I had a red motorcycle with a sick paint job—flames rolling down the side. It was actually just a plastic tricycle with stickers. Either way, those other four-year-old kids in the neighborhood were clearly jealous. My parents had only one rule when I rode this baller bike: do not ride it down the hill to the road. So, obviously, I rode it down the hill to the road. When I came inside, my parents were chill, I thought I had been clever enough to outsmart them. My parents sat me down on the bed, and it clicked that I might not have been as clever as I had assumed.

They simply asked, "Aaron, did you ride the bike down to the road?"

I slyly responded, "No."

Give me a break. I was four and didn't really know how to put together a good teenage lie yet. And don't be reading this all judgmental. You know good and well you were just as sneaky as any other teenager! Anyway, my parents called my foolproof bluff with one sentence: "We saw you ride down to the road, Aaron." I knew my cover had been blown. Of course, I broke under the bone-crushing interrogation and confessed to the crime. The punishment came swiftly and with a belt! However, it wasn't the belt that taught me the lesson that day. It was the look on my parents' faces. I was only four years old, but I learned what disappointment looked like. In the same way, every replay of that day ate away another chunk of Moses's mind and soul. That horrific event looped in Moses's mind, defining him as a disappointment, as nothing.

Often, when we feel as if the mistakes we've made have made us mistakes, we isolate ourselves out of shame. In that isolation, we bear shame never meant for us to carry and listen to lies never meant for us to hear. When we believe the lies calling us a mistake, our minds, just like that of Moses, become the land of nothing. It's the land of nothing because there is no life. There is no life because the lies we believe quench any breath our souls could have. This all creates an isolated mind. Isolation can destroy a mind, and if you lose your mind, you lose yourself.

When we see someone we know hovering in isolation, we tend to believe it's on them to come and ask for help. We see the situation from the side of a loved one there waiting on them whenever they're ready to see the truth. The only issue with this picture is that when you're in isolation, it is impossible to see the truth. Isolation is a dark, long, lonely path. And if you've ever lived in the land of nothing, you understand exactly what I'm talking about.

> *Isolation—the experience of being separated from others—may result from being physically removed from others, as when a person lives in a remote area, or it can result from the perception of being removed from a community, such as when a person feels socially or emotionally isolated from others. ... Taking time to be alone can be a healthy, rejuvenating experience that allows us to reconnect with our own needs, goals, beliefs, values, and feelings. But when a person experiences too much solitude or feels socially isolated from others, he or she may develop feelings of loneliness, social anxiety, helplessness, or depression, among others.*[15]

WHY WE STAY IN DARKNESS

So how can we get so wrapped up in the land of nothing, a land where your mind is held captive and in a constant state of pain? Isolation can stem from many avenues. Often, it is people's doubt in you. Other times, it stems from a lack of self-worth, self-confidence, or even attention or appreciation. I could write pages of lists of the causes of isolation, but if we take the time to dig through the dirt and find the root of the reason, there is one common denominator: your identity has been shaken.

When people doubt you or when you harbor doubt about yourself, your identity is shaken, and your self-worth is low. That's when the lion that is roaming around, seeking prey to devour, comes out to play (1 Peter 5:8). He isn't going to show up when you're strong, stout, and sound of mind. He comes in the dark, lonely times. You know, those moments in the middle of the night when you lie awake, blaming yourself for the marriage that's falling apart, the sin you can't shake, or the bad decisions that haunt you. Isolation didn't trap Moses when he was living in the Pharaoh's palace. Isolation popped its head out of the ground when everything Moses knew began to crumble away. The reason we stay in this dark place is that the darkness of isolation blinds us from the true light available to us.

When Satan was in heaven, he was essentially the worship leader. He was a beautifully created angel and blameless in his ways (Ezekiel 28:13,15).

> *You were in Eden, the garden of God; every precious stone adorned you: carnelian, chrysolite and emerald, topaz, onyx, and jasper, lapis lazuli, turquoise and beryl. Your settings and mountings were made of gold; on the day you were created they were prepared ... You were blameless in your ways from the day you were created till wickedness was found in you.*

He lived in the light of God and brought worship to that light. When Satan was cast out of heaven, his intent wasn't to become the prince of darkness, to be hated for all eternity. He saw how everyone loved to worship the light that was God, and Satan wanted that worship for himself. When God defeated him and cast him away, the desire of Satan didn't change. He desired to be worshiped as light (2 Corinthians 11:14).

> *And no wonder, Satan himself masquerades as an angel of light.*

Satan hates to be viewed as darkness because he is not elevated to the status of God's equal. He longs to be worshiped as God is worshiped. When Satan comes in the night and traps your mind in isolation, your view of him becomes skewed. Satan no longer looks dark and dangerous; he looks comfortable. He no longer has to fight the living light inside of you; he convinces you to shift your mindset from believing that your life is filled with purpose to blaming yourself for each fault of your past. This is what Satan loves.

The easiest action to take in a time of hardship is to blame. Some blame differently than others. You can place the fault either inwardly or outwardly. Both of these courses of action can lead to a rough place. You could blame others by building a wall up around your heart to avoid mistreatment again. Then again, you could blame yourself and bear the punishment of the situation. This option ensures no one can be mad or offended at you, except that you are so miserable inside. The truth is that both of these actions end with the same result—*isolation*. In both of these cases, you shut everyone out. You don't handle the problem in a healthy way; therefore, you become unhealthy. Yes, there are going to be times in your life when you upset someone. You cannot get around that fact, whether it's your parents, your boss, or your spouse. Rather than shoving blame inwardly or outwardly, deal with the truth at the moment. Whether you're putting fault inwardly to yourself or externally to others, the isolation of the situation clouds your mind in darkness. The darkness can overtake you and blind you from understanding the truth of it all. As your mind is wrapped in darkness instead of glorious light, Satan feels he has obtained worship. He can't actually be the light that God is, so he has to deceive us through our minds with the lie that he is good. It's all a lie and an illusion. He uses his deceptive tactics to make it appear that our minds aren't in darkness. He wants us to believe we are in the light because if we truly knew we were in darkness, he wouldn't want that worship. He doesn't want to be worshiped as dark but as light.

If we choose to exercise our faith and see the goodness of God in our isolation, Satan becomes exposed as the darkness he is. If God's light is allowed into our minds and our minds are renewed of who God is and His love for us, the darkness must leave (James 4:7).

Submit yourselves, then, to God. Resist the devil, and he will flee from you.

This explains why isolation is beyond difficult to come out of. The longer you're isolated, the darker your mind. The darker your mind becomes, the more worship Satan feels he is obtaining. He doesn't want your mind to be free because once you're mentally free, he isn't light anymore. He is dark. Once he's dark again, he can no longer obtain his twisted view of worship.

No matter how deep the darkness and no matter the length of isolation, Satan cannot take away your free will. That's where you win! God didn't give us free will in our beings just to see how long it will take us to disobey Him so He can punish us. God gave us free will in our beings so we can recognize the lies and make the conscious decision that we will walk in light and not darkness. We are created to walk our path in fellowship with God and not in isolation from His love.

PEACE ON THE PATH

PAST, PRESENT, OR FUTURE?

Life can become overwhelming almost instantly. We think everything is going just fine until it doesn't. Here's what I mean by that: you're having the most peaceful morning ever. Your devotion was incredible, you have your car pumping your favorite worship, and your heart is elevated beyond anything you've felt before. Then, on the same car ride, you hit traffic. That traffic throws you behind schedule, and if your schedule is behind, nothing good will come out of that day. So you resolve on our way to work that tomorrow will be better. It's not even eight o'clock in the morning, and you're already looking to tomorrow for fulfillment.

It's a popular mindset that if we don't like what our life looks like or where it's going, the only way to be happy in life is to strive for new goals in the future. Yes, it's important to set goals and race toward them. After all, that is the exact point Paul makes when speaking about living life with Jesus as your prize (1 Corinthians 9:24). However, that isn't the popular mindset. The popular mindset leads you to believe that if you don't like where you're at, decide where you want to be and consume yourself with that goal until your life completely revolves around said goal. This honestly seems like the American way, doesn't it? Follow your heart, right? If people find out you're busy and stressed out, they're more proud of you than if things were sailing smoothly. That's because the world views content as stagnant.

What would happen if you did consume yourself with a goal? Here's my story: Before I got married, I had just completed my last semester of college. In the last year of engineering, there was a requirement to graduate called senior design. While the process of senior design teaches hands-on skills that could never be taught in a classroom, it can be more than the mind can handle. This amount of information requires constant attention. One of my college friends said senior design was like a small gnat constantly flying around your head. It's just endlessly buzzing, and you can't kill it. Due to the constant burden of senior design, I forgot everything else in life and focused solely on the project. This caused consistent late nights and tacos at two o'clock in the morning. You don't have to be a nutritionist to know what happened: *a lot* of weight was gained. I was the heaviest I had ever been. It wasn't because I just enjoyed eating. It was because I consumed my life with a burden and lived for nothing else other than that goal. Yes, I was busy, but time is always available if you create it, no matter how impossible it seems. After I graduated, I had accomplished the goal I had set out to do—I got a degree. You would think I felt accomplished, but before I knew it, I dove into something else.

I was heavy and out of shape, and my soon-to-be wife was hot and out of my league. I wanted to look the best I could for my wife when we got married, so I went hardcore on a diet and workout plan—and it worked! I lost the weight I wanted to lose while gaining some muscle. So, once again, I achieved a goal that I set out to accomplish. So why did I feel unfulfilled after I was married? I mean, I had started praying for my wife since I was ten years old with this prayer: "God, I want a wife who loves You like I do, who can help me grow and who is smoking hot." I prayed consistently for that woman for eleven years. So, within six months of my life, I had graduated college with a degree I didn't believe I could obtain, got in the kind of shape I never thought I could be in, and married the literal woman of my dreams. So why was I feeling unfulfilled?

The goals I set for myself were not wrong. It's healthy to have goals. It does good for the soul to have something to work toward and train to obtain. These are good things! But my mindset wasn't right in the pursuit of these goals. I was unfulfilled because I kept looking for the next thing. When I was in my last semester of college, I thought, *If only I could just graduate*. After I graduated, I thought, *If only I could get in shape*. When I was getting in shape, I thought, *If only I could be married*. When I was married, I thought, *If only my career would take a different path*. I kept saying, *If only [fill in the blank], my life would be happy*. I kept looking into the future with a worry that if I didn't take just the right steps and didn't do exactly what I needed to do, I wouldn't have the future I desired. All this did was cultivate constant stress. If we look into the future for our happiness, we will always be unfulfilled. In the same sense, if all you do is look into the past, we will always be disappointed. The past can hold either happy memories that can serve as a green pasture with still waters or a series of doubts and regrets that will be a prison cell for the mind.

So, where *can* we live? If you can't live in the past and can't focus on the future, that leaves only one place: *the present*. It's the most difficult place to live because it's our natural human mindset to be working for something at all times. It's never enough to be content where God has placed you. You must always seek promotions, recognition, and pay raises. You must constantly climb the ladder. But allow me to ask you this: If you're always climbing, how can you ever reach the top?

FRESHLY BAKED BREAD

If I told you there's scriptural proof of living only in the present, you would probably go read the writings of Paul, and Paul is a great reference. However, I'm going to take us to Exodus 16. The children of Israel had been brought out of Egypt, passed through the sea on dry land, and God had slain the very ones who imprisoned them—the Egyptians. How great was their life, right? Well, they didn't think so. They were too hungry and accused Moses of leading them out of the land of Egypt just to die in the desert. They longed to return to the times of Egyptian slavery, because at least then they had a constant food supply. In Exodus 17, they complained to Moses about being thirsty. They accused him of leading them out of Egypt to make them die of thirst. All these complaints came after they accused Moses of leading them out of Egypt to be slain by the Egyptians right before God parted the sea. In Exodus 16, God taught them how to live in the present moment. He rained down bread that tasted like it was soaked in honey. He provided enough that everyone would have three pounds of bread (Exodus 16:16, subnote A). Also, if anyone gathered too little, they didn't have too little (Exodus 16:18). Everyone had just the right amount. There was only one rule: the Israelites couldn't leave any bread for the next day; they had to either eat it all or throw it away. When they did stock up for the next day, the bread would spoil with maggots—not exactly the breakfast I like to wake up to!

Why would God supply inedible bread? Why couldn't they store His provision? God wanted the children of Israel to have trust that He would indeed provide for them and take care of them *every* day. He wanted to teach them that they don't have to give away any worry to tomorrow. As Jesus requests in the "Lord's Prayer," God provides our "daily bread" every morning when we awake (Matthew 6:11).

The bread that was supplied was called manna. The word manna translates to "what is it?" (Exodus 16:31, subnote B). The Israelites had never seen this bread before and didn't know what it was. In the same way that God sustained the Israelites by some unknown substance, God can move in our everyday lives in ways we don't expect or recognize. I'm sure when the Israelites complained of no food, they had an expectation of what God should provide. Something familiar. Something like freshly baked bread made sense. When they walked out of their tents on this miracle morning, when God had basically rained down honey buns from heaven, they were disappointed that what God provided didn't match their expectations. Just because we don't recognize the blessing God is pouring down doesn't mean it isn't what we need. God provided this manna every day for the Israelites until they reached their destination, until they reached their promise.

ASK AND RECEIVE

After God had been supplying fresh, daily bread, the Israelites became thirsty. So, once again, they cried out, accusing Moses. Even though God provided all they needed every day, the children of Israel kept looking for the next best thing from God. Their minds were caught up in this ask-and-receive cycle. This is nothing we can relate to, right? We ask God to provide, and in the midst of God providing, we ask, "What's next?" In this cycle of asking and receiving, there is no room for allowing the Holy Spirit to teach anything. When the Holy Spirit does begin to speak, our misplaced focus on what's to come doesn't allow room for us to hear Him. If we have the wrong focus, we can't hear, and if we can't hear, we can't grow.

The children of Israel continued the cycle of asking and receiving, and they struggled to learn the provision, protection, and nearness of God. When they came upon the promised land, they refused to enter because there were enemies in the land, and they became afraid (Numbers 14). I find this point of their journey particularly interesting because the Israelites were afraid even though God had already shown them His victory when the Amalekites came upon Israel to attack them in Exodus 17 (well before they came upon the promised land). As the Amalekites attacked Israel, Moses stood upon a hill and held up his hands. As long as his hands were raised, Israel would be winning the battle. When he lowered his hands, the Amalekites would be winning. Moses kept his hands raised with a little help from his friends, and Israel overcame their enemy.[16] They wrote about the victory on a scroll specifically to remember this moment of victory. They even built an altar and called it *The Lord Is My Banner*. Israel had experienced the victory of God.

However, the Israelites asked only to receive ("Give us food," "We're thirsty," "Save us from the enemy") instead of listening to hear what God was teaching them. They didn't realize that God was their Banner of Victory not only for one day but for every battle they would face. Israel only learned to receive instead of trust, so when the time came that they needed to depend on God solely to walk into their promise, they could not trust.

REMEMBER AND REGRET

There's another cycle called the remember-regret cycle. This cycle develops due to living in the past. People caught in this cycle aren't the type of folks who remember happy memories and remind themselves of the blessings from God throughout the years. The ones who live in this cycle live mainly in the regrets. They live in the "If only I would have [fill in the blank], I would be happy today." They don't view closed doors as God sovereignly guiding their paths, but they view these instances in their lives as missed opportunities. This mindset will only lead to frustrating disappointment. Since the cycle includes only remembering and regretting, there is no room left for the Holy Spirit to uplift and teach. This cycle can cause you to live constantly down and usually depressed.

People can get hung up on a time where their life, career, or ministry was thriving, and when a new season was issued into their life, they don't know how to handle it. Actually, it was never they themselves who made their life, career, or ministry thrive. It was simply Christ in them. That same Christ is in the transition, too; however, people start to believe the lie that they aren't as "important" as they used to be. They become stuck in a cycle of remembering the times of their thriving life and regretting the time when they walked away, even though they are well aware that it was God's timing. They forget the reason that time of their life was successful: God provided the everyday needs. Fast-forward to the present, and God is still providing the same every day. The only difference now is that the provision is manna; they don't recognize the provision. They didn't learn the lesson of living in everyday trust in God, so now that they're in a time of life when they need to depend on God, they can't. All Christ wants to do in the transitional seasons is take you from one aspect of life to another, but the remember-and-regret cycle blocks the Holy Spirit from moving you to the next glory of your life. The cycle doesn't allow you to receive.

The two cycles have the same end result. Both leave you in a position where your trust in God needs to be developed to move forward in His purpose, but you can't seem to bring yourself to really trust in who God says He is.

HOW DO WE HAVE PEACE?

It's easy on the path we walk not to be where our feet are. We feel the bruises of yesterday and the uncertainty of tomorrow weighing down on us, but when our focus becomes consumed with yesterday and tomorrow, we miss the present completely. How do you have peace on a path that is studded with rough terrain, difficult to navigate, and impossible to predict? You build trust in God, knowing He will provide your daily bread. Whatever the day looks like when you begin to unwrap it—whether it's lonely or full of laughter, pain, joy, birth, or death—build trust. Build trust that believes and knows that whatever comes, the day will not overtake you. God will not allow a day to overcome you.

When the Egyptians changed their minds about letting the Hebrews go, they sent the entire army after them (*terr-i-fying*). There were 600,000 Hebrew men (not including women and children), and they were scared of the Egyptian army (Exodus 12:37). How big must that army have been? Maybe the army wasn't great in number. Maybe the children of Israel were still mental slaves to their former captors. Either way, the children of Israel believed they would be slaughtered. They could not comprehend why God would bring them out of slavery just to die.

Here's the moral of the story: you may not know why the day turns out like it does, but you have to reach out in faith, believing God is providing. Just as the children of Israel could not fathom why they were freed only to be slaughtered, you may not understand why your days keep ending in disappointment, always hoping in the next day only to feel defeated when it comes. But God is not going to put you in a place to be overcome. In the words of Pastor Chris Hodges from Church of the Highlands, "We fight from victory, not for victory." You cannot be overcome, because Jesus has already won the victory, and that same victory lives inside you!

When death was tangible, Moses reached out in faith, and there was a path he could follow. How could Moses reach out in faith in such a trying time? Because Moses had built trust that God would provide when the nation of Israel needed it. The day may be discouraging and seem daunting, but if you reach out in the trust you've built in God, you'll find dry land. You'll find your next step. You'll find peace. God provides manna every day for His children. Nothing is to be stored until the next day. God will provide everything we need for today on this day, and tomorrow, he will provide for tomorrow.

BROKENNESS ON THE PATH

Does this season feel heavy? Maybe you give out all you have until you feel empty. You work day in and day out to feel some sort of purpose, to sense some sort of promise, to achieve some sort of goal. You hope the good you do is enough. You pray the actions you have in your everyday life are directed by the throne room of God. But then, one day, that goal you've worked toward for so long, so tirelessly, comes crashing down. Maybe that day comes when your dream career, that you've worked for years to attain, unexpectedly ends. Maybe it's the day when that child you raised and prayed for so long disregards Christ and rejects everything you worked to instill in them. Whenever that day comes for you, there is one thing in common between us all: that moment breaks you. That moment instantly becomes the most difficult thing ever to forget. But do you know that moment may be the sweetest moment of your life? That moment may be the moment where you're the strongest. It seems like a paradox—I know—but hear me out.

When life lessons are learned through hardships, your soul gets heavy, like the unwanted weight around my waist. After so long, the unwanted pounds begin to weigh on the ground beneath us; our foundation begins to crack. With a weight that becomes heavier and a foundation that is cracking, the only thing left to break is us, and we do. We break, and we crumble to the ground. The weight has won.

When the foundation we stand on breaks beneath us and we shatter, our entire life turns to ruble. So, how do we live now? How do we continue when we feel so hurt, so broken? The unfortunate truth is that at some point of your life, you will break. But the fortunate truth is the breaks in our foundation have a purpose.

BREAKING AND TRUSTING

Make no mistake: breaking isn't fun. Real life isn't like a Hallmark movie; things don't always work out. Times can be tough. Marriage takes hard work, and children have to be consistently instructed in the Spirit to reach their full potential. The careers we are called to take our focus, our relationship with God takes consistent communication, and the list goes on. My point: we don't just wake up one day living our best life with rainbows and shooting stars in the sky. Our life is real, and this real everyday life can rough you up. It can throw punches you never saw coming and storms you never saw forming. This life can hurt us and often leave us raw and vulnerable.

We become a fragile box of emotions, and not everyone handles the box we thought we clearly labeled "fragile" with care. After a few rough handlings, our hearts naturally become calloused. We become jaded and have little trust that those around us will actually handle us with care. Every time our hearts experience this jadedness, we become a little more calloused, our hearts a little more closed. We do this to protect ourselves, but in reality, we accomplish the exact opposite by refusing to allow ourselves to enter a state of trust.

Breaking and trusting walk hand in hand. With every relationship, there can be an action of either trusting or breaking. People aren't perfect. The quicker you understand this, the easier your life will be. I say this because relationships will hurt you, and the closer you get to each other, the greater chance you give another of breaking you.

Sometimes the difference in the relationships that have broken you and those that haven't broken you is simply time.

Even though it feels as if we are the victim when we're broken, often, it's our own calluses that do the damage. But how can the broken be the one doing the hurting? Calloused hearts are simply broken hearts that attempt to piece themselves back together with their own hands. A breaking heart is a delicate thing; if the correct care isn't given to a breaking heart, the heart can end up in a worse state than originally constructed.

If you think in manufacturing terms, God is the manufacturer, and we are the end users, so to speak. God has manufactured an intricate design that is complicated at best. We, as the end users, weren't in the design process, and honestly, we have little clue how to completely and correctly restore the design to its natural state when it is broken. It is easier for us to further break what He has designed than to enhance His design. The design is as fragile as it is intricate. Therefore, the design can be broken with the slightest force. However, the design was premeditated, meaning that God meant to make you the way you are and knew how His design could "malfunction" if tampered with.

Stop for a minute and breathe in the fact that God knew the state you would be in at this moment of your life before you even began walking down your path. He knows every state of the path because He is the path. God understood the factors that would break you just as He understood our sin that broke Jesus as the cross became too heavy to carry. Pay attention to what Jesus tells His disciples about His purpose:

> *The Son of Man must suffer many things and be rejected by the elders, the chief priests and the teachers of the law and he must be killed and on the third day be raised to life. (Luke 9:21–22)*

As Jesus described His purpose, He knew there would be hurt and pain in the death, but He also knew God's heart. Jesus knew His Father wouldn't leave Him in death. He trusted the Father's planned path because God already knew the outcome. The outcome was life, even when it looked like death. God didn't ignore the brokenness and hurt Jesus experienced, and He didn't turn away because heaven was too defeated to respond. He had a purpose for His Son. Inasmuch as Jesus was broken, He was restored. In brokenness, Jesus died, but in restoration, Jesus rose from the dead with sin forever defeated. He was given life when there was brokenness and hurt that resulted in death. So, no matter the brokenness and no matter the hurt, there's an empty grave to remind and to prove that there is restoration. In the hands of God lies this restoration and life. We can't restore our own hearts, just as Lazarus couldn't raise himself from the dead. Jesus spoke life into Lazarus, and with that same voice, He speaks into our sin, brokenness, and hurt to raise and restore us.

God is intentional, and Jesus didn't die by accident. God knew. Jesus was broken and crushed, yes. However, in the sovereignty of God, He was carefully broken, because "the Lord is close to the brokenhearted and saves those who are crushed in spirit" (Psalm 34:18). In the breaking, Jesus trusted in God's unfailing love (Psalm 13:5). There was a breaking in Jesus, but *the breaking came out of trusting*.

So because of this, is God evil? As Paul would say, "not at all." In God's hands lay a plan for His Son's purpose. Jesus was broken, yes, but Jesus wasn't calloused. He sweated blood out of the pain of the process (Luke 22:44), but He didn't close off His heart or become jaded. He pleaded, if there was another way, let that way occur (Matthew 26:39).

> *Going a little farther, he fell with his face to the ground and prayed, "My father, if it is possible, may this cup be taken from me. Yet not as I will, but as you will."*

Jesus wasn't calloused because He placed His trust entirely in the hands of His Father. He didn't attempt to bring Himself back to life in death but rather trusted in the promise God had given Him to complete His path. This action of trusting allowed God to restore Jesus to life as the eternal King of kings in the same moment hell thought it had won. In the same way, our hearts cannot be pieced together when it is in a state of brokenness. Our broken hearts must be surrendered completely to love and trust God to restore. Then and only then will our hearts be restored to a place of wholeness. Where there is no trust, there is no restoration.

Honestly, to the ones going through the breaking, it can feel unnatural to trust when all that we are is shattering. Our lives feel out of control when our foundation breaks, but there is a point to the breaking. There's a purpose to the breaking. God doesn't just allow your foundation to break or for you to shatter without a reason. God allows you and your foundation to break because He then molds you into a completely new masterpiece. When you crumble and your foundation shatters, all that remains are pieces on the ground. This can be the beginning of an amazing thing. With the million little pieces lying on the ground, God freshly molds you so the foundation you once stood on is now inside you. The foundation and truths of God that you once stood firmly on in faith aren't what you stand on anymore, but it's who you are. Who you are and the truths you knew are one. Trusting God in the brokenness allows the truths to be part of you, like intertwined sands—inseparable.

THE VEIL OF BROKENNESS

The moment man sinned, a veil was hung between a holy God and a sinful man. Where there was once a bridge of access between created man and Creator God, there now existed a chasm. This chasm was only crossed by sacrifice and atonement of sin.

> *He shall then slaughter the goat for the sin offering for the people and do with it as he did with the bull's blood: He shall sprinkle it on the atonement cover and in front of it. In this way he will make atonement for the Most Holy Place because of the uncleanness and rebellion of*

the Israelites, whatever their sins have been. (Leviticus 16:15–16)

This veil remained intact until the moment of the ultimate sacrifice—the death of Jesus.

At that moment the curtain of the temple was torn in two from top to bottom. (Matthew 27:51)

There was always a need for a veil and for a sacrifice of atonement between a Holy God and sinful man, until

God presented Christ as a sacrifice of atonement, through the shedding of his blood—to be received by faith. He did this to demonstrate his righteousness, because in his forbearance he had left the sins committed beforehand unpunished. He did it to demonstrate his righteousness at the present time, so as to be just and the one who justifies those who have faith in Jesus. (Romans 3:25–26)

The veil placed between Holy God and sinful man represents lawful actions that cleanse impurities and wash away the sins of man to appear righteous before God. The Hebrew word, translated "atonement," is *kaphar*, meaning "to cover."[17] The act of atonement is to reconcile with God by "covering" what is unholy. The law was to atone for your sins.

The Lord said to Moses, "The tenth day of the seventh month is the Day of Atonement. Hold a sacred assembly and deny yourselves, and present a food offering before the Lord. Do not do any work on that day, because it is the Day of Atonement, when atonement is made for you before the Lord your God." (Leviticus 23:27–28)

This all took place once a year, during the moment when the high priest would enter the Most Holy Place. This Day of Atonement was established because people attempted to enter the Holy Place or attempted to approach God and died (Leviticus 16:1). Still, as a loving God, He allowed a way for the people of Israel to enter in.

> *The Lord said to Moses: "Tell your brother Aaron that he is not to come whenever he chooses into the Most Holy Place behind the curtain in front of the atonement of the ark, or else he will die. ... He must first bring a young bull for a sin offering and a ram for a burnt offering. He is to put on the sacred linen tunic, with undergarments next to his body; he is to tie the linen sash around him and put on the linen turban. These are the sacred garments; so he must bathe himself with water before he puts them on. From the Israelite community he is to take two male goats for a sin offering and a ram for a burnt offering." (Leviticus 16: 2–5)*

Well, no wonder they did this only once a year. It probably took the entire year just to get ready to have the sacrifice. And that's only the first part of the chapter. The rest of Leviticus 16 details exactly what Aaron must do and how he can approach God. It may be hard to see God as loving amid all the rules and rituals. If He wanted a relationship with his creation, why would He put such a religious practice into existence in the first place? It's a simple principle: holiness and sin cannot be intertwined. God doesn't enjoy watching us jump through hoops as many believe; rather, it's because we as humans, in our natural state, are sinful. Instead of turning His back on the people of Israel entirely, God made a way to reach His presence. However, if I had to do this every time I prayed, I would never get anything accomplished in my prayer life. But, if you think about it, isn't this how many of us live out our prayer lives? We take so much time to get prepared and appropriately dressed to enter into the presence of God that we spend little time actually *in* the presence of God, where our lives are changed.

We can make our lives about works and law, which hangs a veil between us and God, or we can walk in grace and freedom, which grants us access to God's throne at all times through the blood of Jesus. When we operate in the law and not in grace, our everyday life looks a lot like the priest's in the Old Testament—always working, always preparing but never experiencing true freedom.

Look at the rich young ruler. The young ruler is asking how to inherit eternal life. This is a good question when asked in the right spirit, out of love for Jesus and not out of greed to continue your own life. Jesus essentially responds, "Do you know the ten commandments?" I'm paraphrasing, obviously. But know this: when Jesus asks you a question, be careful how you respond because He can be setting you up to challenge everything you've ever believed.

The young ruler responds to Jesus, "Not only do I know them! I live by them every day." He's probably thinking at this moment, *I'm golden. I'm even impressing the Lord, who wrote the law.* But then his bubble gets popped.

Jesus said,

> *You still lack one thing. Sell everything you have and give to the poor, and you will have treasures in heaven. Then come, follow me." (Luke 18:22)*

This, of course, didn't sit well with the young man, and he walked away from following Christ. Therefore, am I saying that if you don't give up all your possessions and sell your 85-inch TV and live poor, you can't follow Christ? Not in the slightest. It wasn't because the man was wealthy that Jesus pointed out he should shed his wealth. However, Jesus knew the man was seeking his own betterment and to enhance his own life by putting his life into eternity. His seeking of knowledge from Jesus had nothing to do with actually wanting to follow Christ or even knowing Jesus. The rich young ruler had placed the law on himself to live by and completely missed the point of the law: Jesus. When the moment of decision came to either accept grace or continue in the law, He rejected grace because the law wouldn't permit it.

We can live under the law and be close to Jesus every day and never even come close to Him. The teachers of the law know this all too well because, in Luke, they invited Jesus to eat with them: a meal they wish they never had. The Scripture says,

> *A pharisee invited him to eat. (Luke 11:37)*

Throughout the New Testament, we view Pharisees negatively; they just wanted to see Jesus slip up and trap Him, and that's completely true. But this moment with the Pharisees seemed different. They seemed to desire having dinner with Jesus so they could really understand what He was saying, almost as if there was a moment of decision where they had to decide whether or not to believe in this Christ. When Jesus walks in, He goes to the table and kicks back to relax. It immediately strikes a chord in the Pharisee, who extended the invitation because Jesus didn't wash before the meal.

Side note: with regards to germs, kids, you should wash your hands. Just because Jesus "didn't wash" does not give you the excuse to "be like Jesus." It was more of a ceremonial practice to wash before the meal (Luke 11:38, footnote).[3] Washing wasn't even a lawful practice, just a tradition that the Pharisees added. So, at this point, Jesus wasn't even disrupting the law but just going against tradition. One of the Pharisees had the guts to call him out, so Jesus responded, "Now then …" (You know it's about to get good when Jesus begins with, "Now then …")

> *Now then, you Pharisees clean the outside of the cup and dish, but inside you are full of greed and wickedness. You foolish people! Did not the one who made the outside make what is inside you. (Luke 11:39–40)*

Now tell us how you really feel, Jesus!

> *Woe to you Pharisees, because you give God a tenth of your mint, rue and all other kinds of garden herbs, but you neglect justice and the love of God. You should have practiced the latter without leaving the former undone. (Luke 11:42)*

So one of the Pharisees, who the Scripture calls an "expert in the law," pipes up to inform Jesus,

> *Teacher, when you say these things, you insult us also. (Luke 11:45)*

Now Jesus really finds His stride. "And to you experts in the law …" Jesus doesn't even acknowledge the man's offense but uses it as a tee to drive home another point.

> *And to you experts in the law, woe to you, because you load people down with burdens they can hardly carry, and you yourselves will not lift one finger to help. … Woe to you experts in the law, because you have taken away the key to knowledge. You yourselves have not entered, and you have hindered those who were entering. (Luke 11: 47, 52)*

The footnote of verse 52 says it best: the very persons who should have opened the people's minds concerning the law obscured their understanding by faulty interpretation and an erroneous system of theology. They kept themselves and the people in ignorance of the way of salvation, or as Matthew's account puts it, they "shut the door of the kingdom of heaven in people's faces" (Matthew 23:13, Luke 11:52, footnote).[3]

The Pharisees were the ones with the opportunity to be closest to Jesus. I heard Jennie Lusko say, "Proximity to Jesus does not mean a close relationship with Jesus." The Pharisees believed in the burden of the law, and that's what Jesus points out by saying, "You load people down with burdens they can hardly carry." Jesus presented the Pharisees with the truth. The truth that the law in itself was crushing and that having a relationship with Him was the only way to enter the kingdom. Instead of embracing this truth, instead of accepting this grace that would allow them to carry a lighter load, the Pharisees became furious and hardened their hearts. After all, who was this Man to tell them that the law was wrong? They were the ones who spent years studying it! This is true—they did study it, but they didn't write it.

Like the rich young ruler, the Pharisees held to the law so deeply rooted in them that they missed what the law was originally about: having a way between a Holy God and a sinful man. This Way was sitting right in front of them, and they rejected it. The experts of the law honored the prophets outwardly but rejected the Messiah inwardly. The law is crushing. The law is breaking. Walking with such a burden is difficult! It's near impossible to make yourself presentable, to make yourself polished as Aaron did when he was to go behind the veil at all times. God knows this. God knew the chasm between a Holy God and a sinful man had to be bridged in an eternal manner to have the relationship He desires with His creation. That's what He did by allowing Jesus to come into this world. There was always a need for a sacrifice. Now there is an eternal sacrifice that requires no ritual. In fact, God validates that all of the rituals are needless by tearing the veil that represented the separation between God and man. The veil does not exist anymore. There is no separation. Any lawful act performed in the presence of God is of our own doing, not His. The veil needs to be removed from our own faces because God has already shredded the veil on His side. He sees us for who we truly are in His Son, but do we see God the way He truly is in His love?

> But whenever anyone turns to the Lord, the veil is taken away. Now the Lord is the Spirit, and where the Spirit of the Lord is, there is freedom. And we all, who with inveiled faces contemplate the Lords glory, are

> *being transformed into his image with ever-increasing glory, which comes from the Lord, who is the Spirit. (2 Corinthians 3:16–18)*

GRACE OR LAW?

Do we trust in grace, or do we trust in the law? Do we believe that Jesus's yoke is light, or do we find our relationship with God heavy? If you find it heavy, you are not alone. Many do, because just as the Pharisees, we find it difficult to break the tradition of what we know the Bible to be and know God to be. It is a mindset in which we grew up in, that we lived in, and that most of us currently live in. It's a thought process. The truth is we are not perfect, and as humans, mistakes are going to be made. The truth is that in our weakness, we are made perfect in Christ (2 Corinthians 12:9). We can trust that Jesus is our salvation and purpose. This is the truth, and the truth allows us to be free (John 8:32). But most of us think differently; we don't believe the truth and, in turn, live in bondage.

When we make mistakes, we feel we deserve and expect the punishment of God—not the unmerited, unshakeable favor and love of God. How we structure our thoughts of God can determine whether we break or stay whole. If we accept the latter thought process, we will live in a world of critical imperfection with constant unsatisfactory thoughts and unmet expectations. This is the life and hope of the veil and the law. We will not be able to walk through this life on our own strength and in our own power. This lawful lifestyle is crushing and will break you. If we live in the grace mentality, we can find ourselves in constant contentment and patience in understanding that the absolute perfection of Christ has reconciled all and any troubles we go through or sins we can muster. This is the life of grace. This is the hope of heaven.

Now, when I said, "break or stay whole," understand that breaking isn't wrong, and just because you've been broken doesn't mean you aren't following God's heart. It just means you've built your hope on the wrong source of atonement. Remember, no matter what mindset you live in, God is still loving. God is still good. If the law has been on your life and has broken you, now is a perfect moment to change your life by living in grace. See, when we are broken, we are simply pieces that need to be shaped into something new. This time, instead of shaping ourselves in the spirit of the law, we allow ourselves to be shaped by the perfecting atonement of Christ's grace.

DEPENDENCY ON THE PATH

EXPECTATION AND OUTCOME

I believe that dependence is the most difficult lesson to learn. Dependency, in short, is trust. Trust could be translated to losing all control, all power in a situation, to relinquishing the power of decision in a moment. To put it in a simple analogy, it would be like the old trust exercise, in which you go up on a platform and turn around with your arms crossed and fall back. You are choosing to depend solely on the people below the platform to catch you. What will happen if you start falling back, second guess your decision, and attempt to catch yourself during this trust exercise? One of two things will happen: you will either hurt someone or hurt yourself. If you begin to flail your arms in doubt, attempting to catch yourself, you may possibly smack one of the nice people trying to catch you. Or the nice people might just move because you've lost your mind and are flailing your arms. If they move and you're forced to catch yourself, your arm would probably break. For the trust exercise to work, you have to depend solely on another source besides yourself to keep yourself safe. Again, I believe dependence is the most difficult lesson to learn.

When the Lord moves in your life and chooses to pour abundant blessings on you, it's not hard to accept a blessing. Then there are other times when the Lord moves and pricks your heart to reveal an area of your life where change is needed. As difficult as change is, you're still the one with the decision to change. You cannot change if your free will doesn't allow that change. You're still the one in control of the "change timeline." But when you depend on someone, you lose that control. Just like when we were children, we were dependent on our parents to provide for our needs. However, it's harder to depend on someone else the more responsibility that comes into your life. Because then it feels as if you have a purpose to control situations. We have the feeling we have been waiting our entire lives to be in control of situations, and now, it is our sworn right to control the outcomes. Let's look at this from the aspect of a schedule. When a daily schedule is produced, there are two essential parts: the plan and the outcome.

The top half of the event is the plan. This is the time where the human expectation of the outcome is developed.

Top half of circle representing our plan.

The bottom half of the event is the outcome. This is where the reality of the situation is introduced to our expected outcome.

Bottom half of circle representing the outcome.

The plan and the outcome form to make a circular path. This is a totally normal, human-based thought process. Even if you don't have a daily planner or calendar, there are events every day that we build human expectations for the outcome. Through this process, we develop a routine. We plan the event, the event has an outcome, and the event is closed. We, as humans, are happy with this routine as long as the plan is equivalent to the outcome. However, if the planned outcome differs from our expectations, we sense a ripple in our routine that can cause discomfort. In all moments of this process, we, as humans, are in control. We have a plan, and we have the expectation for the outcome.

Full circle showing plan and outcome

This sounds like freedom, right? You, on your own accord, develop a planned and expected outcome of an event and see through that the event is carried out to your expectations. As much as the world would have you believe that this is indeed freedom, this can also resemble bondage. Please don't hear that Aaron is preaching propaganda that schedules are of the devil and all planning can burn in the home of said devil. Planning and preparing is a great, Godly mindset to have in your life. God blesses you when you prepare yourself to receive what He has for you in His path. But see, that's the key: to receive what He has planned for your path.

Let me ask you a question, please: If you have total control of both the plan and the outcome, where are you receiving God's plan and God's outcome? If the routine of your life consists of your plan and your outcome, this becomes a selfish routine that helps no one and will only bring hurt out of the built-up human expectation.

Hurt? Did he say hurt? *[Goes back to reread the sentence.]* Yep. He said hurt. How could a planned life hurt anyone? That doesn't make any sense. How is being more prepared, being more on time, and being more structured going to hurt anyone? It couldn't. In fact, more people should structure their lives like this, right? Well, I can let you decide that for yourself. Use a parent-child relationship for a moment. Let's name the child Junior and the parent James.

From the moment Junior was born, James had begun developing a plan that would structure Junior's life so he could achieve greatness. James had a timeline something like this:

By the age of four, Junior should be reading slightly above the preschool reading level. After all, above average is what we're all shooting for, right? By age ten, Junior should have developed his oboe skills in which he will excel in the years to come. By the age of fourteen, colleges have been viewed and thought about. By the age of eighteen, Junior has graduated high school (with honors of course) and has been accepted into the college that has been approved by James. That makes sense. James has poured into Junior for eighteen years, so therefore, he is clearly entitled to making a decision that will sculpt Junior's educational betterment to lead to a career path. Junior doesn't know what he wants, anyway. As Junior graduates college, he obtains a job, and after working for two years, he gets married. Over the next five years, Junior will save up money. With this money, Junior and his bride, Elizabeth, will bring a child or two into this earth. James raised Junior, so it makes sense that James would have the most knowledge of when Junior and Elizabeth should bring forth their own child. Junior is then promoted at forty, climbs up the ladder to senior vice president by fifty, and is on the way to early retirement by sixty-one.

In all this, there has been a significant plan and expected outcome. As James predicted what the child would accomplish, there is an expectation set. This is a plan that would set up an endearing life. But what happens if James has planned that Junior should be excellent at playing the oboe but Junior doesn't want to become proficient at the oboe and would rather play football? He's terrible at football, but he is determined to play. So, what do you do? Whether you give in and let him play football or you put your foot down and make him play the oboe, there is going to be an expectation that is not met. James gives in and lets the kid play football. The hurt isn't too bad, but James does have a sting in the heart where Junior rejected his plan. At fourteen, instead of looking at colleges, Junior is more interested in hanging out with his friends. Once again, a failed expectation. When he turns eighteen, Junior does indeed graduate high school, but most certainly, he does not with honors. James is disappointed slightly because he knows it was mainly Junior's lack of focus. A little more adds to the pain of unmet expectations. Next, college. This is the time where James finds out instead of going to class, Junior has returned home in the middle of the week, in the middle of a semester, to let James know that he is now "exploring himself." This time a deeper wound is made within James because Junior is now blowing any opportunity that he once had just because he is lazy. Once again, Junior disappoints because there was an expectation not met. Junior then gets married without a degree and unstable income. James smiles, but his heart is broken for his child. At every milestone moment, Junior becomes something other than what

James expected. James still, of course, loves his son and will never stop loving him, but when the opportunity presents itself, it may be good to let Junior know that the love is there with a hint of disappointment.

For instance, at the Thanksgiving dinner, when Junior is talking about a difficult time he is having at work, James pipes up to remind him, "I know it's difficult, but it will pass. This is why I wanted you to get a degree." There is supporting love in that sentence, but it has an aftertaste of disappointment. The statement of love is coated in selfish agendas. This isn't the only time this type of statement happens, though. When James and Elizabeth have their own baby, they complain about how tired they are, but James reminds them, "This is why I wanted you to wait until you were twenty-six instead of twenty-one to have a kid. You would've been more prepared." There is still love in that sentence because James truly wanted only to make Junior's life better. Because James himself was young once too and knows how hard it was on him and his wife having a baby at twenty-one years old. Still, this is a statement covered in disappointment. Through all the disappointment-coated statements of love, Junior begins to feel defeated from the burden of disappointment. Junior does what is natural, and he pulls away from the source of the burden. Junior begins to pull away from James. It may begin by not telling the parent about small issues because Junior knows James expected something different. Throughout Junior's life, every time he attempted to speak to James about an issue he was facing, he felt only disappointment from the less than constructive "love statements."

The saddest part of this relationship is that the expectation never met the outcome from either side of the relationship. There is now a chasm between the heart of the parent and the heart of the child. What was once a relationship that connected at a creation level has now become severed. Both Junior and James are rigid. They each saw their plan as the only plan.

A plan for a life is a good thing. It does provide stability and a goal to race toward; however, the plan wasn't the problem, was it? The problem was how James and Junior both dealt with the disappointment of the other breaking the plan. The rigidity of a full circle plan has come and gone and no one is the better for it. In fact, both parties are now hurt and require to seek restoration and council to remove the heartache. Once again, it isn't the plan itself, it is the rigidity to depend solely on that expected plan instead of depending on the plan of the good Father.

SWAY WITH IT

If I'm honest, having our life plan messed with by undetermined, unforeseeable factors can be brutal. However, the only thing we can accurately predict in life is that there will be unpredictable circumstances. But how do we deal with the unpredictable circumstances? How do we change from rigidity to dependence?

I believe the best example of dealing with unpredictable circumstances is how tall buildings in large cities are constructed. These huge structures that seem to be so tall that they touch the sky would have to be a solid, rigid structure to withstand the forces that nature may throw at it, right? Actually, no. These large buildings don't stay still—they sway. If the buildings had no sway to them and were completely rigid, the building wouldn't last. Eventually, the building would snap under the pressure of the environment.[18]

Life is going to throw unpredictable circumstances your way, and there will be moments in life that are the exact opposite of what you expected. If you are so rigid in the planned outcome, there will be a snap at some point or another that will cause hurt to not only you but others around you. If a tall building snapped in a large city, don't you think that would bring some destruction to the surrounding buildings?

It is unequivocally necessary to depend on the Father to guide your plan and allow the Spirit to alter the plan you have made. What happens if you hear the Spirit say, "I don't want your son to play the oboe"? But you have a determination for oboe playing because you played the oboe, like your dad before you, or whatever weird tradition you have in your family. Are you going to tell the Spirit, "No"? The life of the child was never yours to plan out but the Lord's, for He gave the child its breath and purpose.

This is similar to when Jesse didn't even bring David when Samuel asked to see the sons of Jesse. David wasn't supposed to be King because he wasn't worthy. He was simply a shepherd and nothing more. Well, Jesse's plan was incorrect. David became the King that other Kings exemplified. Abraham didn't plan to take a hiking trip with his son to sacrifice him, but he allowed the Spirit to alter his plan as the Spirit said so. Since Abraham was flexible to the Spirit and depended on the Father's plan rather than his own, Isaac was spared and went on to birth nations. The way to change the selfishness of planning, expectation, and receiving your outcome is dependency.

Dependency is simple in conception but incredibly difficult in execution. However, I believe dependency is the key to allowing the sway in our rigid lives. When dependency in God is introduced, it allows room for the Holy Spirit to move in between our plan and our outcome to introduce God's purpose for our lives.

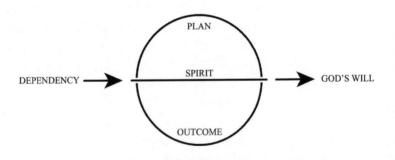

Allowing the Holy Spirit in our plans and outcomes.

PROVISION

Dependence can be uncomfortable. It's a process where we learn how to conform our minds to think in the exact opposite way of our natural state. Our nature is to work with the expectation that provision will follow. What if provision is indeed exactly the opposite? What if provision has nothing to do with the works you do? What if provision actually has nothing to do with you? This is an awkward and uncomfortable way for our minds to think, and Jesus knows this. That's why when Jesus taught us how to pray. He addressed how to pray about provision. In Matthew 6:11, Jesus prays,

Give us today our daily bread.

If you're like me when I was younger, I knew Jesus would give me all the white bread I wanted, but what about the real food? Where is the sustenance? That's cool. You have an unlimited bakery, Jesus, but what about my car, my groceries, my scholarships? In the difficult, stretching moments of our lives, we begin to wonder, *Is He going to provide in this moment?* Or we think, *If He does provide, will it be enough to make ends meet?* God our Creator knows this human-nature mentality and how all of these anxious thoughts weigh us down, but yet, all He teaches us to pray about provision is, "Give us today our daily bread." It is almost such a small prayer about the provisions of this world that it's easy not to take this part of His prayer as a promise. This part of the prayer can make us feel the most uncomfortable. It is in this part of the prayer where we lose total control and place all responsibility on Christ. The line directly before the request of provision says,

Your kingdom come, your will be done on earth as it is in heaven. (Matthew 6:10)

This line of Jesus's prayer prepares our hearts to release control of providing our own provision to completely allow *all of Jesus into all of our needs*. It is a request of God to provide for us in all we need, in whatever measure we need it, all in His timing.

Let's break this down. Humanity has a constant need for dependency whether or not we would like to admit it. Every day as we arise, we have an immediate need for provision. Those needs may vary for different people, but at the very basic, those needs are oxygen, water, food, shelter, and sleep.[19] With those five items, even though it may not be glamorous, you could survive, right? Our human bodies are frail. Even the strongest of men can be ended by a simple sharp object. Our voices are beautiful but can be taken away if we talk too loudly for too long. We have so many vulnerable areas as humans if our constant need for dependency isn't met. Day in and day out, we depend on something to provide these needs.

This world offers several areas of provision. If you need some time to breathe, just hop on the spinning wheel of social media and take a ride only to have the breath sucked of you. You need water? Come to the well of hope, where we place all expectations and dependency in immediate satisfactions to quench our thirst, only to long for something more. As far as food and shelter are concerned, grind harder than the person next to you so there is more for you when it comes time to consume. After all, the harder we work, the nicer shelter we can afford. Whatever you do, don't share the wealth you've made, and don't allow people to steal what you have rightly worked to hold. Ah, and sleep. There's really no time for it, but if you must squeeze in a couple of hours, we have sleeping pills and anxiety medicine that, once popped, will remove all the concerns and worries placed into your life. I'm of course being sarcastic here.

This is how we typically live our lives. Stressed and simply depending on the next immediate provision to protect us and make us feel secure. It's the American dream. Yet somehow, despite all the fillings of this world, we need breath, we thirst, and we depend. But Jesus knows our frailty; we are made out of unsustainable dust (Psalm 103:14).

> *For he knows how we are formed, he remembers that we are dust.*

This is why He teaches us to pray about provision. He knew what this world does to the human mind and the weight it can place on you.

Doesn't He say, "In this world you will have trouble" (John 16:33)? Did He not then know about the pressure and tribulations that we live under—the second job we need, the extra shift we need to pay rent this month, or simply the chaos in our minds we call everyday life? And even if we conquer a day, we have to fight the war again the next day. As soon as we find the water of this world, we become thirsty from the journey to find it. Just as quickly as we find room to breathe, we awake to a new alarm for a new day that begins to squeeze our hearts and restrict our minds like a python around its prey. Our Jesus knew all these pressures that require us to have a daily dependency. That's why He teaches us to pray, "Give us today our daily bread." Every human need we have, there is a daily provision to meet that need. Before the day begins and before that alarm of pressure sounds, provisions have already been made to make you prosperous and victorious.

USELESS DIRT

Before man was created, God looked at dust and had an idea. God looked at the dust and breathed life into it (Genesis 2:7).

> *Then the Lord God formed a man from the dust of the ground and breathed into his nostrils the breath of life, and the man became a living being.*

He breathed life into what most people would call useless, and the human race began. The same is true for us. Before your day begins, God looks over your life and sees what you have to offer. He sees the potential of the seeds He has planted in your life. He sees what others may be calling useless and starts to breathe life over it. And if we allow it, life begins to form. Our allowance is key; we choose how much the seed of God will bloom in our lives.

The Hebrew word in Genesis 2:7 is *afar*, which could be translated to "dirt" or "soil."[20] Therefore, we could say that God breathed life into dirt or soil to make us. And if we are the soil, we determine how much nourishment the seed that God is planting in us receives.

The spirit of God has made me; the breath of the Almighty gives me life. (Job 33:4)

Before we even have time to worry about the pressures of the next step on the path, God takes the ground of the path, the dirt or "useless" and hopeless situations in our lives, and breathes life on it to give us life! The provision is, therefore, simply the path on which we walk—even if it seems useless or hopeless. God has planted a path of purpose into our lives before we were even conceived. If we choose to follow the narrow path that allows God's perfect will to happen "on earth as it is in heaven," He will provide for our human dependency and give us the strength to follow Him on this path. For He is the path. He is our past, present, and future. Was He not the God who "was, and is, and is to come" (Revelation 1:8)? Will He then not know the provision you have needed and will need going forward? My point: it's not on us to provide! The pressure isn't on us to perform well enough to obtain these things. He is the provision, the breath, and the water, and in Him, we fulfill our dependence.

RENEWAL

When understanding dependency, the most important thing to remember is that *God doesn't change*. So if God doesn't change, if He has a purpose and a plan and has already thought out our provision for that purpose, why would we ever lack anything? Romans 12:2 states,

Do not conform to the pattern of this world, but be transformed by the renewing of your mind.

What is this verse saying? God doesn't change, but we do. In our human dependence, our minds can gravitate to the next-best provision of this world, but we must take authority of our mind and focus our dependence back on the Father, who loves and gives freely. It's so important to renew our minds so we remember to pray, "Give us this day our daily bread." To remember that every day God has enough, and God is enough. For if we walk on the path of His creation, there is already provision built into the path of His purpose to meet all our needs. When we need breath, He is the breath in our lungs (Job 33:4). When we are thirsty, He gives water that will never leave us wanting ever again (John 4:14).

> *But whoever drinks the water I give them will never thirst. Indeed, the water I give them will become in them a spring of water welling up to eternal life.*

When our souls need to be fed, He is the most filling bread (John 6:35).

> *Then Jesus declared, "I am the bread of life. Whoever comes to me will never go hungry."*

When we need rest, He's a safe, strong tower to lean on (Proverbs 18:10).

The name of the Lord is a fortified tower; the righteous run to it and are safe. Simply put, God is everything. There is nothing He cannot provide, and because He is good, He "will meet all your needs according to the riches of his glory in Christ Jesus" (Phillipians 4:19).

Once again, I believe dependence is the most challenging lesson to learn. To live in a mindset of dependence, we must have a heart of a child (Matthew 18:3). This seems unnatural. We must surrender our adult privilege of controlling situations to our satisfaction and learn the same dependence we were taught to forget. It may take time to learn this dependency. Moses spent forty days in a cloud with the Holy Trinity before he understood what his lesson was (Exodus 24:18). It may take longer for us, or who knows? Maybe all God has to say is one word, and you got it!

God may place us in circumstances where we are completely uncomfortable so we learn, *in all our ways*, to depend on Him (Proverbs 3:5). Dependence can unlock a new level of your relationship with God.

My dad always told me the most important thing you could ever say in a relationship isn't "I love you" but rather "I trust you." Why is that? You can love someone to the moon and back and do everything for them, but do you trust them enough to be still and let them go to the moon and back for you? Would you be all right giving up that control? In our relationship with God, we have to trust and depend that He is the One who is guiding our steps along the way.

There was a time in my walk with God that I became incredibly concerned, near paranoia, that the next step I took wouldn't be in His will. I worried that if I didn't hear His voice and completely understand, I would miss what He had for me. However, God isn't sneaky. He doesn't make it complex with a list of vague rules that say if I don't completely do as He says, I'll be voted off the path. If God truly is an all-loving gracious God, how could I miss His will? Think about Paul for a moment. Before Saul was Paul, he hated Christians and everything associated with a new radical movement about a man named Jesus. Saul was actually traveling to Damascus to arrest and punish those who believed in Jesus. On his journey, Saul was blinded by Jesus, and his life was forever changed (Acts 22:6). Paul wasn't even interested in God's purpose for his life, and he didn't have to go seeking to find it. So, how much more could you find God's purpose if you are seeking it?

If there are doors in your life to which you feel a draw—it could be an idea, a new invention, or even a career change—don't be afraid to push on that door to see what happens. If you trust God and are walking in His purpose for your life, depend on Him to keep the doors closed that you don't need to be walking through while opening the exact specific doors you are supposed to walk through. God has proven throughout His Word that He is dependable and good in all His ways.

> *And we know that in all things God works for the good of those who love him, who have been called according to his purpose. For those God foreknew he also predestined to be conformed to the image of his Son. ... And those he predestined, he also called; those he called, he also*

justified; those he justified, he also glorified. (Romans 8:28–30)

It isn't our plan, our outcome, or our provision that will lead us where we need to go or give us what we need. But a daily renewing of our minds to allow *all of Jesus into all parts of us* will provide all we need, in whatever measure we need.

CHOICE OF THE PATH

THE DILEMMA

One beautiful Sabbath morn, Jesus rolled up to the synagogue to spout a little wisdom of God on some folks. During His teaching, one of the attendees appeared to be different from the rest of the crowd. He stood out to the crowd because of his deformed hand. He also stood out to Jesus as well, but for an entirely different reason. Let's keep this point in mind: it was the Sabbath. This is important because it was unlawful to do works on the Sabbath. Got that point locked in? Need me to say it again? Good. The Pharisees, shockingly, were trying to trap Jesus in the rules of man, but Jesus doesn't work within the boundaries of man's limitations. Jesus understands the rules, and He knows what the Pharisees believe, so obviously, He has no respect for those rules. In the middle of the synagogue, Jesus decides to destroy the ritual boundaries that the Pharisees have set. He looks at the man with the deformed hand and says to him,

Get up and stand in front of everyone. (Luke 6:8)

When Jesus looks at this man and tells him to stand up, there is no telling what is truly going through this man's head. What could he have been thinking? We can only speculate, but I know a few things that might pass through my mind. Place yourself in this situation. Close your eyes. Never mind—open them. I guess it's kind of hard to keep reading with your eyes closed. Anyhoo, paint this picture in your head: You have always been viewed as less than others. You've always been made to feel as if you were incapable of performing at the same level. Maybe this isn't so hard for some of us to imagine. However, even in our circumstances, we keep striving. We show up to church, grab our coffee in the foyer, and head to the sanctuary. We have to get someone to open the door for us, though, because we have the coffee in our strong hand, slightly reminding us again of our insufficiencies. We take our place, we engage in great worship, and we are ready to hear what that cool speaker has to say. He doesn't speak all the time, but we like what he has to say because something about Him. It just seems as if He has a sense of freedom no one else can figure out. It doesn't make sense, though, because He doesn't obey all the laws the leaders around me enact and insist we obey. During His speech, He pauses for a moment and looks into the corner of the room. It's unclear what He was thinking, but He looks at the leaders, who are standing in the corner, paying specific attention to His every action. Even though they are watching so closely, you can tell they aren't really listening. It's almost as if they're just staring through His words to make sure He doesn't mess up the tradition we have here at church. The speaker then sighs, turns His head, and looks straight at us. He says, "Get up and come down here to the front." We aren't sure He's really talking to us, so we do a double take behind us only to turn around to the Speaker, verifying He did mean us. What could he want? Why would He pick us? He has influence. Is there something that we did? Did we break a law? We swallow the knot in our throat and step over the nice family to our left. Get in the aisle and begin the walk down to the front. The heart pounds, and we begin to oddly sweat in weird places. We feel incredibly uncomfortable. We get to the front and look up at this Man.

When this man stands up, Jesus commands the man,

Stretch out your hand. (Luke 6:10)

Remember the fact that this is the Sabbath? It's a big deal because it was not permitted to heal on the Sabbath. Jesus is going against the rules and the understanding of man. These people knew the Sabbath was a day of rest and understood healings were not permitted.

The Speaker looks into our eyes and says, "Stretch out your hand." We stare back at Him in shock. What should we do? Did He just call us out to bring us up here and embarrass us because of our insufficiency? Oh! Surely, He wants to use us as an example, a teaching object, so He would want the strong hand, right? It's been only a second since He's commanded us to stick out our hand, but it feels like ten minutes with the conundrum weighing in our head. Wait. This is that same Jesus, the One who performs all the miracles. Surely not! He wouldn't put us in this situation. He wants to heal us on the Sabbath. That's not allowed; I'll get arrested! Two seconds have gone by. Isn't this guy supposed to be the Son of God? If He is, then again to the point that He would want us to stretch forth our best quality. If He is who He says He is, wouldn't God want our best?

Three seconds. In this moment, this man was faced with what probably seemed at the time to be an impossible situation, with no good outcome. I can relate. I've been in situations where I felt God was standing there waiting for me to make a move, but feeling on the inside God didn't really understand what He was asking of me, that He would end up costing me.

We continue to weigh the situation and think, *Then again, if this Jesus heals the paralyzed, maybe He wants to accept my weakness.* So, in the largest trust we've ever found, we begin to lift the hand, which is shriveled and basically useless. As we stretch the hand out, we realize something. We can squeeze our hand. Oh, what? Our hand is transforming before our eyes. The hand has changed! It's larger and stronger than our strong hand. Four seconds.

THE PROCESS

When the man stretched out His hand, "his hand was completely restored" (Luke 6:10). Why does Jesus heal this man's hand? Why did his hand then have to be restored? Was it simply to perform another miracle? Maybe it was deeper than a healing.

This man in the synagogue was presented with a decision that could shape the remainder of his existence. Several factors needed to be taken into consideration. If he does trust this Jesus, which is probably what he wanted to do in the first place, he could be healed. On the other hand, he could go back to his seat, operate in what is comfortable, and have the approval of his leaders and those around him. This decision was heavy. One decision could lead to a temporal but immediate life of approval. The other could lead to eternal approval but possibly a long, lonely life. This decision isn't one that would be taken lightly, and there was a process of this man making a decision.

It wasn't as simple as Jesus speaking and the man doing. There were mental mountains to overcome even to allow himself to stretch forth his hand. This would have been a lot easier for the man if Jesus simply came up to him, grabbed the hand and healed it, and then told the man to show everyone the miracle that had just been performed. Jesus, instead, calls the man to "stretch." Why would He do this? Would the healing not do just as much without calling out the man? Simply put, the act of stretching produces faith. If Jesus gave the man healing without the man moving on his end, what would the man have gained? Yes, the physical result would have been the same—the man's hand would have been healed. However, what do we know about Jesus? He wants a relationship. So, if this man obtained healing without stretching, his heart would have been the same. There would have been no growth of trust between that man and Jesus. And it probably wasn't only the man's heart that was healed; the act of stretching likely affected the hearts of everyone around him.

Deciding to stretch is no easy task. All eyes are on you. Will you trust this Man who calls you to stretch outside your normal range? You can feel the pressure of the moment, and rightly so. If you do reach out, this Man could heal you and completely change your life, but there is always a fear of "what if?" What if He won't change your life? What if He does change your life, but in all the wrong ways where your job, your way of living, or family dynamic changes? If stretching was an easy process, everyone would be walking in their perfect calling and in perfect peace with Christ.

Three Gospel accounts recall the moment where Jesus healed this man's hand. "Why there's not four of them, Heaven only knows."[21] Randy Travis folks will catch that one. All three accounts give an example directly before this moment of another Sabbath in which Jesus ticked off the Pharisees by disrupting their lawful Sabbath. Jesus had a Sabbath too, but He had a graceful, not lawful, Sabbath. He says in the Gospel according to Mark,

> *What is lawful in the Sabbath: to do good or to do evil, to save life or to kill? (Mark 3:4)*

He says in Matthew,

> *If any of you has a sheep and it falls into a pit on the Sabbath, will you not take hold of it and lift it out? (Matthew 12:11)*

He presented a question to the crowd but directed at the Pharisees, to test and see if they were obeying traditional law or the love of God. In each account, when Jesus presented this question, no one had a response. Their hearts probably knew the answer, but their minds couldn't let the love of God stretch their hearts to see a perfect truth. There were not just mental mountains for the man with the withered hand to climb but also everyone around him who was a witness. Clearly, the nature of the situation was to shut the love of God off before it could interfere with the laws of God. The action of this one man being willing to stretch started to change that. Because of his availability and willingness, Jesus could do a miracle in a place that He was never allowed to before.

YOUR WEAKNESS IS SPECIAL

Why would Jesus call this particular man, though? What made him special? It was his weakness. This man's inabilities allowed Christ the room to move. God has a very difficult time moving in the areas of our lives that we are strong because we don't believe we need a miracle in those areas. However, when we can see our weakness with our own eyes, we are much more open for someone to step in and change our lives. When Jesus said to the man, "Stretch forth your hand," I believe Jesus was saying, "Stretch out what you have. Stretch out the weakest part of you. If you stretch out what you have, I'll change hearts and alter the hearts of a religion." So many people want the miracle to happen in and around their lives, but hardly anyone wants to stretch for it. They expect the miracle to come with their strong hand, and their strong qualities stretched out, and their crippled hand hid behind their back. But Jesus says to stretch out the crippled hand. Stretch out the hand that holds the depression, the bad decisions, the regrets, the heartache, and the past mistakes. Stretch out the hand that is shameful. God wants to do something so great in the rooms you have influence in, but it requires you to stretch out your hand. The room of the synagogue couldn't have changed that day if the man wasn't willing to stretch out his hand. Why would Jesus, as you are standing there among all your people of influence, request that you present Him with the weakness in your life? Because in our weakness, He is the strongest (2 Corinthians 12, 9–11).

COMMIT AND CHANGE

After we climb some mental mountains, and when the time comes that we do stretch out our weaknesses, we have to commit. There can be no second doubts. The stretching is a process. We don't know what process the man had to go through in his heart and in his mind that day. There were others in that room that would've said, "Don't you dare. You can't receive what that man wants to do. This isn't how we live." That's why you have to commit. You have to be committed when the people of influence in your life would argue against it. You have to commit when the people around you would condemn you. So many people miss the point of knowing God. They become so consumed with a commandment God gave them that they ritualize and regulate God. They miss out on the actual point of it all: Jesus. It's complete speculation, but perhaps the man stretching out his hand allowed for other hearts to see Jesus as Messiah. Stretching hurts, and it's embarrassing and uncomfortable. But if you do stretch, what can it open? What world could you change if you committed and stretched the crippled things in your life to the One who will heal and transform? So the question is this: Will you be willing to stretch?

FEAR OF THE PURPOSE

THE GRIND

The world says you are created for the chase. It is filled with things that demand your attention and your efforts for minimal reward. This is typically the cycle most of us live in. We live in service to this world to gain our dreams. I believe, if I'm correct on my young man slang, these days that's called "staying on the grind." We grind and grind so we can accomplish our dreams and make it to the top. The only thing this world fails to let you know before you start this journey: there is no top. You will climb the rest of your life and never make it to where you "want to be." At least not for long, because as soon as you make it to where you dreamed, someone else tries to take your spot. You get back to grinding simply to keep that other person from taking over your dream, to prove to yourself you're worthy to have your dream. In short, the grind exists simply so you don't miss out. What if you slip from being on top? Will you have the things you do now? Could you ever be as happy as you were on top?

The grind is deceptive by nature. It produces endless effort with little reward. Essentially, the grind never stops because there is no top.

After a while, this world begins to entangle you in a debilitating grip of what you could miss out on. The grip is slow but becomes tighter every time you gain something else off of the grind. Over time, the more success produced of your own hand, the more debilitating the grip becomes, debilitating to the point where you forgot the reason you even wake up every day, because you've been chasing an unfillable, unpleasant void. We spend our entire lives trying to fill and please this void, but it's so deep, we can't seem to ever close the gap. Before we realize, we've forgotten who we are. We don't remember why we're here. All we know is that there is a void that needs filling, and no one can fill it but us. We long to fill this void to the extent that filling the void becomes our unspoken purpose in life. We wake up every morning with the intention not to feel that void when we go to sleep that night. Some call this motivation. However, the more we chase this void, the tighter the grip becomes. Eventually, we get to the point where we cannot breathe on our own anymore. We become dependent on the feeling that there is something to be earned and our performance will dictate how much we gain. This dependency ends up becoming our identity. It all happens at a fast, exponential rate.

If I can be honest with you, I was recently in a position where I realized I was chasing the wrong thing. My life felt like chaos, and I had no control over how the day went. My days felt extremely dark. I don't say this for your sympathy, just so you understand that this is real. I felt terribly afraid that my performance wouldn't measure up and the value I had just wouldn't ever be enough. I lost my identity.

Identity can come through what you're in a relationship with. I believe it's important to understand that we can get so caught up in doing things for God that we forget why we are doing them. It's easy to think this isn't for us, because our life isn't about works. We know God. We're always in church, leading a small group, or stacking chairs like the humble servant we are. But just because you're doing things *for* God doesn't mean you *know* God. You can serve a church your entire life and never know the Father. That's why no matter how many times you do work for God, the void you feel inside never seems to close. If you think God is more interested in what you can do for him instead of just being His child, you have it all wrong. He desires a relationship with you.

One day as I was praying, I felt the Lord say, "Why do you live in fear of missing things that you were never meant to have?" In that moment, everything became clear. I was trapped in the grip of fear that was blinding me to the truth. I was spending so much effort trying to chase a void and reach a place I was never meant to reach. So many people spend their entire lives climbing a mountain they were never meant to climb and then wonder why their life always felt like a struggle. Understand, this could be in many areas of your life: work, relationships, or your major in school. We become caught up in fear of not having "it" that we begin to allow this fear to control our actions and decisions.

IT'S NOT ABOUT YOU

In 1 Samuel 9, Saul was anointed the first King over Israel. The anointing placed on Saul in this time signified a "separation to the Lord for a particular task and divine equipping for the task" (1 Samuel 9:16, footnote).[3] Saul's purpose as king of Israel was to deliver Israel from the Philistines (1 Samuel 9:16). Saul didn't come from much, and most would call his life an OG rags-to-riches story. Saul was a humble man who woke up in the morning and was assigned to find his father's lost donkeys (1 Samuel 9:3). In no way was Saul expecting to be anointed, much less anointed king by the end of the trip. When Samuel told Saul that he would be king, Saul replied,

> But am I not a Benjamite, from the smallest tribe of Israel, and is not my clan the least of all the clans of the tribe of Benjamin?" (1 Samuel 9:21)

The selection of a king didn't make much sense to Saul, but he accepted. As time went on with Saul as king, there were several moments in which Saul took matters into his own hands. In 1 Samuel

13, Saul was standing opposite the Philistines, and all the Israelite soldiers were terrified (1 Samuel 13:7). Rewind back in time to chapter 7: Samuel sacrifices a burnt offering to the Lord before a battle against the Philistines; the Lord fought for Israel, who destroyed the Philistines (1 Samuel 7:9–11). In chapter 10, Samuel instructs Saul to wait on him to sacrifice a burnt offering; then Samuel would then tell Saul what he is to do (1 Samuel 10:8). So, as Saul stands before the Philistines, Samuel hasn't shown up yet, and his soldiers begin to scatter (1 Samuel 13:8). So, in fear of waiting and the feeling of responsibility to defend Israel, Saul neglects the Lord's command and offers up the burnt offering himself. When Samuel shows up, he scolds Saul telling him that he had done a "foolish thing" (1 Samuel 13:13). In a time of fear, Saul took the responsibility of the anointing upon himself to fulfill a void instead of depending on God to deliver what He promised.

God didn't appoint Saul to rule over Israel as a true King but be an instrument that would allow the purpose of God to unfold in Israel. That's why as Saul took the responsibility of the king and defender over Israel upon himself out of his own ambition, Samuel told him,

> *The Lord has sought out a man after his own heart and appointed him ruler of his people, because you have not kept the Lord's commands." (1 Samuel 13:14)*

Over time, Saul sees God's anointing shift from himself to David. This puts a fear in Saul that he may lose his position (1 Samuel 18:12).

> *Saul was afraid of David, because the Lord was with David but had departed from Saul.*

Saul then does everything in his power to place David in positions to fail so Israel would see Saul as more powerful than David. A little side note: often, people above you will place you in positions of hardship beyond your experience so you can fail and they look good. However, no one can stop what the Lord has begun (Romans 8:31). In the same sense, David was successful against every challenge because he was operating in God's anointing while Saul was operating out of fear of losing what he was never meant to hold. This fear changed Saul. Saul, at one time, was zealous for God and wanted to listen to the instruction of the Lord, but with the fear of losing the throne clouding his mind, his entire personality changed. Saul was anointed King; that was not a mistake. But Saul could not be used anymore because his entire focus shifted to the position of power rather than positioning himself to listen and obey God. Saul felt the control he desired leaving and wanted to stop David from allowing God to use him. Saul knew he wasn't living in the right spirit (1 Samuel 15:24).

> *Then Saul said to Samuel, "I have sinned. I violated the Lord's command and your instructions. I was afraid of the men and so I gave in to them."*

However, Saul just couldn't stop himself. He had more of a desire for retaining what God had for him in the past than receiving what God could've had for him in a future season. This is complete speculation, but who knows how else Saul could have been used if he would have simply not given into the fear of losing control? It could have been nothing, but it could have been something more than pursuing a man that he was never able to kill, only to kill himself. God had a sovereign purpose that Saul couldn't see, but Saul trusted only what he could see. All Saul saw was a young kid taking his place. He didn't see a lineage that would introduce Jesus into the world. Saul forgot to realize the most important thing: *it was never about him.* It's the same in all of our lives. We feel we have personally earned the position we sit in, but it couldn't be further from the truth. Wherever we are, God placed us there. That's why there's no position too high or too low that God cannot use. Saul's downfall came because he lived his life attempting to fill a void that was never his to fill instead of serving God in the purpose that God had placed him in.

CONTROL AND PERCEPTION

Living to fill a void is restless and self-serving. Living in purpose is contentment and serves another. Living to fill a void will allow a slow gripping fear to take your life and transform it to where you control nothing; the lack of control causes anxiety. Living in purpose will also remove your control, but the lack of control causes trust.

Living in fear of lack comes out of a place of desiring control. We understand that if we have and hold on to what we desire, then we're in control of our lives. However, this fear overwhelms our lives so much to the point that we only live to gain and never to give. Before we realize it, we begin to live in a fear that we will lose one of the precious things we worked so hard to gain. This loop is endless, and it makes our lives feel like chaos. It makes us feel as if we have no control. But think about it, did we ever actually have control? Grinding to obtain the world only gives the perception that you have control in your life. It's a facade. I know this is true. After all, how do you feel the moment one thing is removed from your life you worked so hard to obtain? You feel as if the world has just crashed down around you and stolen your control. Then again, wouldn't the lack of control also be a perception?

The point here is that perception controls everything. I heard Steven Furtick, the pastor of Elevation Church, say, "Reality is just your perception." If I took a poll of a church audience and I asked, "Who here would say the purpose you're walking in is playing out exactly how you expected it to?" you would get a few hand raises, for two reasons. One: they're liars. Two: they haven't actually taken the chance to go to a deeper point in God's purpose, so there is no opposition. If everyone were honest, though, no one would raise their hand. What God calls us to rarely feels like the purpose of God we expected. Think about any story in which God's purpose unfolded and the individual walking through the purpose completely understood what was happening at every event. You may spend a while looking for that one. Walking in God's purpose rarely turns out the way we expect it to.

Mark 4:35 begins a short but highly taught passage in which Jesus tells His disciples to "go to the other side." As the boat is traveling, a storm hits, and the disciples are terrified. You can sense their fear since they go to Jesus during this moment and ask,

> "Teacher, don't you care if we drown?" (Mark 4:38).

Jesus calms the storm and responds,

> "Why are you so afraid? Do you still have no faith?" (Mark 4:40).

In the heart of the storm, the disciples had forgotten the reason why they were going to a new destination. Often, we can get into the middle of the purpose God has called us to and forget why we're even following this path. Why would Jesus ask these guys, "Why are you so afraid? Do you still have no faith?" Jesus was trying to show them that no matter the circumstances and no matter what life looks like, have faith. Jesus didn't bring the disciples to the middle of the water to drown. Jesus had a purpose. Jesus had a point of getting through the storm. On the "other side," there was a man who desperately needed Jesus. This man was demon-possessed and lived in isolation—exactly where Satan wanted him. But Jesus went through the storm and into this man's isolation to rescue and restore him. Even in the disciple's fear of crossing the water in the storm, Jesus was right there with them. The journey to the other side wasn't what the disciples expected, and they began to panic and fear. Fear begins to creep into our lives when our perception doesn't meet our expectations. Jesus didn't see the storm and suddenly realize that He had made a terrible mistake. He just had a sovereign viewpoint to the storm that the disciples didn't have.

Levi Lusko, the pastor of Fresh Life Church, once said, "Fear is often thought of as a noun, not a verb." I find this quote fascinating.

We treat fear like it's a person, like it has a reason and a purpose to be in our lives. In reality, fear and faith are both verbs that we can choose to activate. Every morning, there is a decision to make as we begin our day—will we choose fear or faith? It's a simple question but has the power to determine your entire life.

TESTIMONY OF THE PATH

If I'm honest with you, this book isn't words of wisdom from someone who miraculously heard the voice of the Lord and inspirationally wrote a book. This book was written in a time where Jesus had to continuously speak into my life and remind me of His goodness. When I say in this book, "You aren't alone," I truly mean that. The experiences you've had in your life that result in dark, hard, and challenging times aren't just happening in your life.

> ...*You know that the family of believers throughout the world is undergoing the same kind of sufferings (1 Peter 5:9).*

We all are walking our path with the loving Father, and He is there in all of our situations—no matter how many and no matter the difficulty.

I began writing this book in a time of hardship. I was a recent graduate of college, and I was in my first year of employment. I landed an extremely well-paying job, so you would think I was living the American dream, right? Go to college, get a degree, and become wealthy. From the outside, perhaps my life seemed like one others could envy, but I was actually envious of them. Turns out that job wasn't all I expected it to be. Long story short, the job shook every part of me to my very core. Everything that I had ever known was falling apart. Anything I held my identity in gradually fell out of my life, and very few days went by without another person telling me how useless I was. These things happened every day until all that was left was simply the rawest form of me I'd ever been. I was exposed in every facet of my life. I had always been someone that people could see have faith in circumstances, but honestly, it was always easy to have faith when everything worked out in the end. It was different knowing this time that my situation wouldn't work out as I thought it would. For the first time, I truly didn't have control, and I was terrified. I was a failure.

This may seem like an extremely dark moment of my life, and it was. The moment was dark because I kept my focus on the situational circumstances and not the sovereign goodness that God had on my path. God wasn't allowing me to simply go through misery. There were things in my life that needed to be broken, and unfortunately, I was stubborn. But once I began to surrender to God's purpose and what he sovereignly saw in my life, I had peace with the situation. Even though I had surrendered to God's plan, the situation didn't change. Honestly, I still kind of cringe when I think back on that time of my life. However, my focus began to shift ever so slightly into what God's plan was and not what man had in store for me. Shifting my mind allowed God into the situation. I could have prayed all that I wanted and for as long as I wanted, and believe me, I did. I prayed every day to be removed from that situation, but until I allowed the truth of God to enter, I stayed in my misery. The moment I began allowing God into my life, everything began to change. This may sound like a happy ending to a short story, but the change that occurred wasn't a good change by human standards (A.K.A, I got fired). However, the change was necessary in my life for me to walk on the correct path God had for me.

The following year, I could feel God's chisel chipping away at me every day, as if I were His sculpture. And the chisel hurt. The more God formed me into what He has called me to be, the more I was forced to look at myself in the mirror of truth. My dad always told me that if you want to see who you truly are, look into a mirror, because you can't hide the truth from yourself. Everyone else around you may see you for the happy, carefree person you portray, but you know the deep hurts and secrets no one else does.

A few months later, my friend called me up and asked if I wanted to come to a worship night at his house and just have a house church service. I'm a big fan of that kind of stuff, so I went, but little did I know that night would begin a work in me I couldn't imagine. Toward the end of the night, my friend asked if anyone had anything to share. I spoke up. Meanwhile, in the back of my head, I could hear a voice saying, "Stop talking! No one here wants to hear whatever nonsense you have to say. You don't even make coherent sense."

Has anyone else ever heard that voice, or is it only me? I kept talking even though I could hear my heart pounding in my head, and after I spoke, a man from across the room whom I had never met looked at me and said, "You're brilliant." This was incredibly uncomfortable for me. I'm terrible at taking compliments, especially when I know they're coming from God. Others started speaking up, saying, "You're beautiful. You're bold." At this point, I was just thinking, *Dude, don't you dare cry!* Some people there that night had known what I had gone through, and others had no idea. Regardless, God saw the broken pieces of my life and my mind, and He was determined to show His love to me. I had always struggled with knowing how much God loved me, almost as if I would put a salary cap on his love based on how well I performed. The people there laid hands on me and began to pray. They prayed over my mind, and I began to see Jesus standing in front of me, saying, "Do you know how much I love you?" I had never felt such an overwhelming love in my entire life!

After we had prayed, my brother-in-law spoke up.

"Aaron, I just want you to know what God has shown me. You've been looking into a mirror and seeing what you think is yourself, but Satan has been on the other side of the mirror manipulating what you see. But God has taken your attention and shown you what you look like to him, which is blameless perfection. He has shattered the mirror."

I had been looking at my life and my purpose in a mirror in which Satan had manipulated to look like failure. My life wasn't a failure. I was simply walking in obedience. Sometimes failure isn't the reason things don't work out. Sometimes, it is simply you being obedient to God's path. Obedience and failure can look identical to the world, and Satan will use that to make you believe you're not enough and that you could never measure up. But know that is a lie. God had a plan for your life before you were even born.

> *Before I formed you in the womb I knew you, before you were born I set you apart. (Jeremiah 1:5)*

God has ordained sovereignly-thought-out steps for every turn along your path. The steps may not seem ordained because we see and feel the hills and the valleys of our path, but we can trust that the steps are ordained. God planned your life out way before you were even thought of, and when He looks over your life, He doesn't see a dense 3D forest with large mountains and rugged terrain. God sees our life as a 2D map. I don't mean that God isn't in our every moment as we walk this path, because he is, and I am not saying God is distant from our side. I say this because as we feel the high and the lows and the hard times and harder times, God remains constant.

God isn't affected by the circumstances of our lives. God still feels our hurts and our brokenness because He is a close and loving God, but His faithful goodness doesn't change as our situations change. Even though every mountain seems like a never-ending journey and every valley seems as if it can take you out of God's view, God sees us just the same, whether we are high on a mountain or low in a valley, like 2D vision. The depth of our circumstances doesn't change the way God sees us. As we walk this path He has created for us, He sees the path from a sovereign perspective. He sees where we are on our path and how we get to the end of it. If we can only let go of the frustration of conquering mountains and the fear of what's in the next valley, we can lift our eyes and see that God is above all and is in control of all we do. We only have to trust the Creator of the path more so than the conqueror (us) of the path. If we shift our focus from conquering the next season of our lives to obeying and learning from the One who created where we are in our journey, we see that our path wasn't created to serve ourselves. Our path was created to advance and serve the ministry of Jesus. God sees us where we are and knows how the end of our path ties into His sovereign, eternal plan. There is purpose on the path.

PATH PRAYERS

If you're reading this and wonder who this Jesus is and would like to get to know Him, I want you to know that He is right here waiting for you. Just pray this and open your heart:

> *Jesus, I believe what your Word says about you. I believe You are the only begotten Son of God, that you died for my sins, and that you rose from death and are now seated in Heaven with the Father.*
>
> *I would love to know you better. So, I simply invite you into my life to show me who You are and to be Lord over all of me—to have the final say in every decision I make. Come into every part of my life.*
>
> *I confess that I've done things without you for a long time. I've made mistakes and decisions that are not honoring to You. Forgive my sins. I'm sorry. I choose to submit to You over my own desires. And as I confess my sins, I thank you for forgiving every single sin according to Your Word.*

Have my heart. Have my life. Walk with me and show me who You are.

In Jesus name I pray, Amen.

Maybe you've read this book and you know Jesus quite well. You walk with Him, talk with Him, but still things are heavy and burdensome. Maybe you've walked on this path for a long time with Jesus, but you aren't sure of your next step. You feel stuck and have no idea what to say or how to pray. I want you to know that you aren't crazy. You aren't alone. Jesus sees you; He understands the burden.

Lord, I confess you as that—my Lord. Which means that you get the final say. So, I may not know what to do or which step to take, but You do. So be the Lord of my every step, have the final say, and lead me in the way that is everlasting. In the name of Jesus I pray, Amen.

WORKS CITED

1. Unless otherwise noted, Scripture quotations are taken from The Holy Bible, *New International Version, NIV,* Copyright 1973, 1978, 1984, 2011 by Biblica, Inc.

   **All scriptures in this book are taken from the NIV version unless specified otherwise.

2. Scripture quotations marked THE MESSAGE are taken from *THE MESSAGE.* Copyright by Eugene H. Peterson 1993, 1994, 1995, 1996, 2000, 2001, 2002. Used by permission of Nav-Press Publishing Group.

   ** Scriptures in this book only where notated.

3. *NIV and The Message Parallel Bible.* Copyright 2013 by Zondervan

4. Maxwell, John. *Developing the Leader Within You 2.0.* Harper Collins Leadership, 2018.

5. *Gilmore Girls*, The WB/ The CW, 2000-2007. Netflix

6. Scripture quotations marked KJV are taken from KJV Gift & Award Bible, Revised, Copyright 2002 by Zondervan

   ** Scriptures in this book only where notated.

7. Parsons, John J. "Be Still and Know That I Am God." *Be Still and Know That I Am God*, 2020, www.hebrew4christians.com/Meditations/Be_Still/be_still.html.

8. Kids, Posted By Engineering For, et al. "News." *Engineering For Kids*, 7 Oct. 2020, engineeringforkids.com/article/05-25-2016_

Arch-Bridge-Facts. http://engineeringforkids.com/article/05-25-2016_Arch-Bridge-Facts

10. "Arch Bridge—Types of Arch Bridges." *Arch Bridges—Facts and Types of Arch Bridges*, 2020, www.historyofbridges.com/facts-about-bridges/arch-bridges/.
11. "Arch Bridge." *Wikipedia*, Wikimedia Foundation, 6 Oct. 2020, en.wikipedia.org/wiki/Arch_bridge.
12. "Theoretical: Definition of Theoretical by Oxford Dictionary on Lexico.com Also Meaning of Theoretical." *Lexico Dictionaries | English*, Lexico Dictionaries, 2020, www.lexico.com/definition/theoretical.
13. Rutland, Mark, *David the Great*. Charisma House, 2018
14. Scripture quotations marked NLT are taken from the Holy Bible, New Living Translation, copyright 1996, 2004, 2007 by the Tyndale House Foundation.

    ** Scriptures in this book only where notated.
15. Team, GoodTherapy Editor. "Isolation." *Learn about Emotional and Social Isolation, Treatment For*, GoodTherapy, 2018, www.goodtherapy.org/learn-about-therapy/issues/isolation.
16. Beatles, The. "With a Little Help From My Friends." *Sgt. Pepper's Lonely Hearts Club Band*. Calderstone Productions Limited (a division of Universal Music Group), 2009, track 2.
17. Stetzer Bio, Ed, et al. "A Closer Look: Jesus and Atonement in the Old Testament." *The Exchange | A Blog by Ed Stetzer*, 2012, www.christianitytoday.com/edstetzer/2012/january/closer-look-jesus-and-atonement-in-old-testament.html.
18. Harris, Tom. "How Skyscrapers Work." *HowStuffWorks Science*, HowStuffWorks, 9 June 2020, science.howstuffworks.com/engineering/structural/skyscraper4.htm.
19. Sleight, Kenneth. "List of Five Basic & Immediate Needs for Physical Human Survival." *Https://Www.brighthub.com/Environment/Science-Environmental/Articles/123273/*, 15 Aug.

2011, www.brighthub.com/environment/science-environmental/articles/123273.aspx.

20. H., J. (2011, May 06). What is the Dust of the Ground from which Man is Formed? Retrieved October 31, 2020, from https://goddidntsaythat.com/2011/05/06/what-is-the-dust-of-the-ground-from-which-man-is-formed/amp/

21. Travis, Randy. "Three Wooden Crosses." *Urban Cowboy*, Word Entertainment LLC, a Curb Company, 2002, track 5.

22. *"prepare" in WordSense.eu Online Dictionary (28th December, 2020)*

23. *Saturday Night Live*, NBC, 1975-Present.

24. *Indiana Jones and the Last Crusade.* Directed by Steven Speilberg, performances by Harrison Ford, Sean Connery, Alison Doody, Lucasfilm Ltd., Paramount Pictures, 1989.

25. Cedarmont Kids, "The Wise Man Built His House." *Silly Songs*, 1995

26. *Cabul Definition and Meaning - Bible Dictionary.* biblestudytools.com. (n.d.). https://www.biblestudytools.com/dictionary/cabul/.